HOLY LISTENING

HOLY LISTENING

The Art of Spiritual Direction

Margaret Guenther

DARTON·LONGMAN + TODD

First published in 1993 by
Darton, Longman and Todd Ltd
1 Spencer Court
140-142 Wandsworth High Street
London SW18 4JJ

Reprinted 1994, 1996, 1998, 2000, 2002, 2004, 2008, 2010, 2012

ISBN 10: 0–232–52008–9
ISBN 13: 978–0–232–52008–8

A catalogue record for this book is available
from the British Library

Most of the Scripture quotations
are taken from the Revised Standard Version of
the Bible, copyrighted 1971 and 1952 by the
Division of Christian Education of the National
Council of the Churches of Christ in the USA.

Phototypeset by Intype London Ltd
Printed and bound by CPI Group (UK) Ltd, Croydon, CR0 4YY

CONTENTS

FOREWORD

SOME YEARS AGO, a monk responded angrily (but with a twinkle in his eye) to a lecture I had given on spiritual direction. I don't think he was mad at me or even at the subject matter. It was the trendiness of it all that got to him. He said, 'What I want is some non-spiritual non-direction!' He had a point. Spiritual direction can easily become too 'spiritual' in the sense of being ungrounded and unreal. It can become too directive by either being overly clinical or authoritarian. There is always the danger of the well-meaning or spiritually bossy charging into someone's life uninvited and doing some real damage. Some of us like to dabble in other people's lives and thus enlarge ourselves by interfering.

Spiritual direction needs demystifying and Margaret Guenther goes a long way towards doing just that by writing a wise and penetrating book about non-spiritual non-direction. She has managed to throw light on the ordinary ground of everyday human experience out of which extraordinary acts of spiritual courage and perseverance are born.

In some ways, the art of spiritual direction lies in our uncovering the obvious in our lives and in realising that everyday events are the means by which God tries to reach us. When Molière's *Bourgeois Gentilhomme* discovered that all language was either poetry or prose, he was delighted to learn that he had been speaking prose all his life without knowing it. So with us. All along we've had a spiritual life and we didn't know it. There *is* poetry in the spiritual life but most of the time we are living in the prosaic mode.

Margaret Guenther knows a great deal about the strange ministry of gracious human interaction that the tradition calls the midwifery of the soul. She also knows that writing about spiritual direction can be hazardous. It has become a mini-industry in religious publishing. This is all right in itself. The danger lies in the fact that it is well-nigh impossible not to be infected by the prevailing attitudes of an acquisitive, competitive, and consumer society. These attitudes even permeate our approach to things spiritual. Prayer is one more thing one has to *do*, one more skill one has to learn in order to run the spiritual race and get ahead. For some, having a spiritual director is like having your own therapist or your own personal trainer at the gym. It gives one spiritual status. It promises a spiritual edge over others. Having a spiritual director is like moving out of the inner city of the spirit and into the suburbs where there are more facilities and the promise of a membership in the country club of the soul. Having a spiritual mentor will make you spiritually upwardly mobile.

Another debilitating effect of the drive and greed of a consumer society on the life of the spirit is the assumption that everything is, in principle, **fixable**. True spiritual direction is about the great unfixables in human life. It's about the mystery of moving through time. It's about mortality. It's about love. It's about things that can't be fixed. Margaret Guenther knows about the great unfixables.

Talk about spiritual direction can, therefore, be very irritating. It's not so much the subject matter per se as the fact that when we talk about anything 'spiritual' resentment, jealousy, and guilt are often stirred up in people – partly because we are haunted by the spectre of unfixability. If someone implies that he or she has anything approaching a disciplined spiritual life, some of us get a sinking feeling inside. We either compare ourselves unfavourably with the other person, or we look for the flaws that must be hiding under the veneer of piety.

What kind of person, therefore, should be writing about the spiritual life today? She would need to be very grounded in ordinary, everyday experience. She would need to be earthy and have the ability to see the funny side of the spiritual enterprise even in the midst of great suffering. She would need to be crafty – wily enough to spot the byzantine ploys of the ego to make itself the centre of everything, even of its own suffering and struggle. She would need to be able to make judgments without being judgmental, to smell a rat without allowing her ability to discern deception sour her vision of the glory and joy that is everyone's birthright in God. Margaret Guenther is such a writer. She is also a feminist, that is, she writes from the perspective of a woman who has known what it is to be made invisible and to be set aside, ignored and unheard.

There's a lot of daft talk about the need for 'a woman's perspective'. One writer recently told of the way in which she was always called upon for 'the woman's point of view' in graduate school. It became an in-joke with her friends: 'Speaking as a woman, I think I'll have meatloaf for dinner.' Yet there *is* a much-neglected feminine perspective that is at last being heard. Margaret writes a great deal about listening, waiting and presence – all attributes that are associated with the feminine. She is unafraid of using images traditionally associated almost exclusively with women – metaphors of housekeeping and house-cleaning. But she pulls no punches when she takes on patriarchal attitudes and posturing. When it comes to matters of simple injustice and plain ecclesiastical nonsense, she is both critical and inclusive.

Spiritual direction is very susceptible to the female imagery of pregnancy and birth-giving. God is the great birth-helper. It is no wonder that midwifery is the overriding metaphor of spiritual direction, and Margaret Guenther insists that men are as capable of it as women. We assist at the birth of each other in an environment of gracious hospitality. We also, from time to time, act as parents to each other. When a formerly autistic child was asked what parents were for, she replied, 'They hope for you.' That is what we can do for each other.

But there is more to be learned than the recovery of the feminine in the use of metaphors from midwifery. There is also the recovery of the role of older people (the elders) in bringing souls to term. Grandmothers and grandfathers can play an important part in soul-making. Margaret conjures up the image of the Appalachian granny woman – wise, resourceful, and experienced – assisting at the birth of babies in cottages and shacks remote and hard to reach. We need spiritual grannies and grandpas who have the time and the wisdom to wait patiently in out-of-the-way places of the spirit and quietly bring new things to birth in others.

Men and women have common sins but they also have ones very much identified with their particular sex. The traditional sin is pride and it is still very much alive, but, according to Margaret Guenther, the sin that clings particularly to women is that of self-contempt. Man's pride and woman's self-contempt (while not exclusive to either sex) make relations between the sexes unusually sour at the moment. Perhaps that is why both men and women invoke a high and cruelly idealistic standard of behaviour that only superbeings could uphold. Modern secular standards of morality are draconian compared to the old-fashioned religious standards which, at least, held out the promise of forgiveness. Most of us make a fundamental error with regard to the nature of morality iself. We all want a workable framework of rules in a fixable world that most of us can follow without any real effort. We like things to work, including our morality. So we try to manoeuvre ourselves into a morally secure position by changing the rules. The new rules are either a device to punish the politically incorrect or they are so inconsequential that human relations are trivialised.

There is another point of view that this book will do a great deal to revive. This other perspective is best illustrated by reference to a story of an encounter between a Catholic convert from communism and one of his old atheist colleagues. 'The difference between us is that I believe in absolute responsibility and absolute forgiveness. You believe in no responsibility and no forgiveness.' Human life isn't worth living without our willingly accepting responsibility for our behaviour, yet that would be too heavy a burden without the possibility of forgiveness. Those of us who hope for a more caring and humane world had better be aware of forgiveness (both human and divine) if we are going to navigate the stormy seas of human relations. Much of the pain could be avoided if we knew how to frame questions about our longings and were willing to forgive one another, even as we seek to make one another accountable. Spiritual direction, at its best, does just this.

The spiritual director has the double task of holding up the demands of absolute responsibility and the promise of absolute forgiveness. It is out of such demands and promises that we assist at each other's birth. Margaret Guenther knows what it means to grow into being someone. There is waiting, stillness, and hope. 'When in doubt,' she writes, 'I always assume that God is at work, that is, the person is pregnant.' Just as she found it useful to refer to *The Complete Book of Midwifery*, so her readers will find this book an invaluable manual in recognising God's amazing work in us and among us in the ordinariness of human existence. In the very best sense, hers is a book on non-spiritual non-direction: earthed and wise, compassionate and unsentimental, practical and contemplative. May more of us be willing to seek hospitality with another in the art of birth-giving.

Alan Jones
Grace Cathedral, San Francisco

INTRODUCTION

THIS IS A BOOK by an amateur, written for amateurs. Amateur – a word devalued in our time, connoting someone not to be taken seriously, not quite up to snuff, certainly a poor (but usually inexpensive) substitute for the worthy professional.

Yet the amateur is one who loves, loves the art that she serves, loves and prays for the people who trust her, loves the Holy Spirit who is the true director in this strange ministry called spiritual direction. The amateur is nervous about hanging up a nameplate or taking an advertisement in the Yellow Pages. The amateur waits for others to name his gift and may find out quite accidentally his calling to this ministry. With Abba Macarius of the fourth-century Egyptian desert, who protested, 'I have not yet become a monk myself, but I have seen monks,'[1] the amateur-lover-director may say, 'Who, me? I have not yet become a spiritual director myself, but I have seen spiritual directors. Or at least read about them!'

It is a strange ministry, often exercised in the interstices, intruding itself into the practicalities of parish administration or sermon-writing or teaching. Sometimes I am almost reluctant to name it, for the very words – spiritual direction – can be offputting or seductive, as they conjure up the image of a clerical Svengali compelling a trembling soul to kneel on broken glass while reciting the Miserere.

The terminology may be the best we have, but domination and submission are **not** what spiritual direction is about. When people ask what we do here at the Center for Christian Spirituality, I occasionally hedge and think, 'If you have to ask, I certainly can't tell you.' Reflection on the ministry of presence and attentiveness make me remember Mrs G from my days as a

---

[1] Benedicta Ward, *The Desert Christian: The Sayings of the Desert Fathers* (NY, Macmillan 1975), p. 125.

hospital chaplain. A formidable woman, who looked quite a lot like the Red Queen in *Alice*, she was seriously ill and – with her ceaseless demands – a source of annoyance to the nursing staff. One day after I had fetched her glasses and found her teeth, adjusted the television and repaired the Venetian blind, put fresh water in her pitcher and plumped her pillow, I assumed that Mrs G had run out of urgent needs. But she beckoned me close and said, 'One more thing. Get me out of here!' When I protested that, much as I would like her to be well, granting this particular request was out of my power, Mrs G looked at me with disappointment and some disgust. 'You mean you just walk around and listen to people?' I felt very small and very fake when I answered, 'I'm afraid that's it, Mrs G.' A slow smile crept over the Red Queen's face. 'Well, I guess that's work, too.'

I don't walk around much any more, but I still listen a lot. And I often think of Mrs G, who probably never heard of spiritual direction but would no doubt grudgingly recognise that 'it was work, too'.

Paradoxically, the need and hunger are there, even as we struggle to define the ministry. Cursillo has brought the words 'spiritual direction' back into currency, but most lay people and many clergy are uneasy and unsure of their significance in the late-twentieth-century Church. We are hungry, and we don't know for what. We want something, but we can't name it. The parish is taking good care of us, nourishing us with word and sacrament, just as the hospital made sure that Mrs G was fed, nursed and medicated. But we want something else, something more: we want to be touched, we want to be known as children of God. So we behave spiritually like Mrs G, all too often missing the point and assuming that adjustment of the external environment will somehow fix everything. Yet what we really hunger for is wholeness and God.

The spiritual director may be tempted to fix things, to be diverted as I was diverted by Mrs G's teeth and glasses, television and window-blind. To combat such temptation it is good to remember the spiritual maxim offered by the American novelist John Irving in one of his books: when you help people, you mess with them. Anthony the Great had a similar idea over 1600 years earlier, when he quoted Abba Paphnutius as saying, 'I have seen a man on the bank of the river buried up to his knees in mud and some men came to give him a hand to help him out, but they pushed him further in up to his neck.' Anthony commented approvingly of Paphnutius: 'Here is a real man, who can care for souls and save them.'[2] Whatever we do as spiritual directors – and with God's help – we neither mess with them nor push them further into the mud.

Yet the hunger is there, and some of us – lay and ordained – find ourselves asked to respond or at least to be present. Again and again, people call the Center for an appointment 'to talk to somebody'. There is urgency in their voices, and they are often surprised that no one can see them that very day, that it might be necessary to wait a week or two. Then, when they arrive, when the door is finally shut and the phone turned off, they say apologetically, 'I'm not really sure why I'm here. I don't know what I want.' They want God, of course, but they aren't able to say so. They want to know themselves in relation to God, but they aren't able to say that either. They want spiritual direction, but that too they are often unable to say.

Direction is not psychotherapy nor an inexpensive substitute for such therapy. Yet the fields are compatible and frequently share raw material. Nor is it pastoral counselling although, again, there may be compatibility and overlap. Finally spiritual direction is not to be confused with the sharing that takes place in deep friendships, for the direction relationship is unashamedly hierarchical. Hierachical not because the director is somehow 'better' or 'holier' than the directee, but because, in this convenanted relationship, the director has agreed to put himself aside so that his total attention can be focused on the person sitting in the other chair. What a gift to bring to another, the gift of disinterested, loving attention!

In this book I will attempt to describe the shape that spiritual direction might take for people of our time, aware that the subject is an elusive one and that spiritual direction can have many faces. While one is always gratified by the attention of one's colleagues, my words about this potentially intimidating subject are directed to the beginner, those persons lay or ordained, with or without formal theological training, who find themselves drawn to this ministry. Perhaps they feel the stirring of their own unacknowledged gifts. Or perhaps they wonder about receiving direction, whether it is a ministry available to 'ordinary people' or reserved for the specially holy. I hope some dark corners will be illuminated and some questions answered. As an amateur I can write only from my own perspective.

First and foremost this is the perspective of a woman, and a

[2] Ibid. p. 7.

woman who has been married for over three decades and has
borne and brought up children. Most of the major recent books
on spiritual direction have been written by men – the names of
Alan Jones, Morton Kelsey, Tilden Edwards, William Barry
and William Connolly, Kenneth Leech, and Martin Thornton
come immediately to mind – although Edwards points out that
women appear to have special gifts for this ministry:

> The dominance of men is another obvious reality. My sus-
> picion is that there are many more great women spiritual
> guides than the record shows, but who have remained in
> obscurity in the normative dominance of men in the pos-
> itions of visible leadership. Hopefully, this 'negative learn-
> ing' from Church history will be corrected in our time. My
> own experience points to more potentially gifted women
> than men as spiritual companions.[3]

Further, a number of the women who **do** write on the subject
are members of religious orders and hence speak from a different life experience and viewpoint. My life as a woman, wife and
mother has given my ministry its particular shape.

I also write from the perspective of a teacher, as one who has
spent a lifetime entrusted with the minds and lives of students.
I have always been aware, at some level, of the holiness of the
teacher's vocation. With each passing year the connections
become clearer to me: teaching is indeed ministry, and much
ministry – especially the ministry of spiritual direction – is
teaching.

Finally I write as a priest of the Episcopal Church. When I
first sought ordination I was sure that my ministry lay with the
dying, most probably in the institutional ministry of hospital,
nursing home or hospice. To find myself again in academe
seemed at first ironic to me, a sign of divine humour, but upon
reflection very right. I do indeed work with the dying, for we
are all dying, and helping in the preparation for a good death
is priestly work.

From this perspective, I hope, will emerge one person's
vision of spiritual direction. It is a vision with three aspects,
blending into one another, yet separate: spiritual direction as
hospitality, teaching and midwifery.

[3] Tilden Edwards, *Spiritual Friend: Reclaiming the Gift of Spiritual Direction* (NY,
Paulist Press 1980), p. 67.

To be asked by someone to serve as his spiritual director is an awesome expression of trust. My immediate reaction is almost always the inward question, 'Am I up to this? What makes this person think that I am worthy of his trust?'

It is my hope that in this book trust has not been violated and that my pledge of confidentiality has been observed. But this work would not be possible without the very real people who sit with me in my office or who ask for conferences during the retreats and quiet days which I conduct. Because of them I am not writing about what spiritual direction might or should be; rather, I am writing – often anecdotally – about one person's ministry as it really is.

All the stories I have told are **true** but not necessarily **factual**. No real names are used, circumstances have been changed and composites created. Since this is a book about 'ordinary' direction situations there are many commonalities. While each person seeking direction is unique, there are recurrent motifs, problems and concerns. The **sameness** is far from boring; it is part of the human condition, binding us together and enabling us to feel kinship with the great spiritual writers, once we have got past the superficialities that make them seem remote.

I am deeply grateful to my directees, my spiritual children who are my brothers and sisters, my fellow travellers, my friends. I thank all of you: women and men; gay, lesbian and straight; tentative seekers and confident theologians; young and old. If you think you recognise yourself in these pages, you do – and you don't. In some instances, when the story becomes very specific and the material is delicate, I have secured your permission. In others your story is here, woven – I hope – seamlessly and discreetly into the fabric.

1

SPIRITUAL DIRECTION
AS HOSPITALITY

He lifted up his eyes and looked, and behold, three men stood in front of him. When he saw them, he ran from the tent door to meet them, and bowed himself to the earth, and said, 'My lord, if I have found favour in your sight, do not pass by your servant. Let a little water be brought, and wash your feet, and rest yourselves under the tree, while I fetch a morsel of bread, that you may refresh yourselves, and after that you may pass on – since you have come to your servant.' So they said, 'Do as you have said.' And Abraham hastened into the tent to Sarah, and said, 'Make ready quickly three measures of fine meal, knead it, and make cakes.' And Abraham ran to the herd, and took a calf, tender and good, and gave it to the servant, who hastened to prepare it. Then he took curds, and milk, and the calf which he had prepared, and set it before them, and he stood by them under the tree while they ate. (Genesis 18:2–8)

Practise hospitality. (Romans 12:13)

Do not neglect to show hospitality to strangers, for thereby some have entertained angels unawares. (Hebrews 13:2)

Never give a hollow greeting of peace or turn away when someone needs your love. (Rule of St Benedict, Ch. 4)

Let all guests who arrive be received like Christ, for He is going to say, 'I came as a guest, and you received Me.' (Rule of St Benedict, Ch. 53)

Those who receive you receive me, and those who receive me receive the One who sent me. (Matthew 10:40)

EVERY MORNING my day begins with a look at the little black appointment book. Usually the space is crowded with names and phone numbers, and the shape of the day is predictable. But occasionally the name scribbled in is unfamiliar to me: someone is coming for the first time, presumably to explore the possibility of spiritual direction, but even that is not always clear. I'm not always sure how the person found me – a suggestion from the parish clergy, a casual reference by a friend of a friend, the mysterious spiritual grapevine, or even the New York telephone book. Despite a preliminary phone conversation to set up the appointment, we are strangers to each other. Names without faces or stories.

I am about to show hospitality to a stranger, a prospect simultaneously exhilarating and disquieting. I become aware of myself – perhaps they are expecting someone older, younger, taller, shorter, at least someone who looks like a spiritual director. While my friends and colleagues are used to my office with its books and pictures, perhaps the stranger will be put off by it. And what about the stranger himself? What does he want of me? Will he be interesting, tedious, challenging or – this is, after all, New York – possibly deranged?

These thoughts do not always run through my mind in clear sequence, but they are just beneath the surface when a potential directee presents himself for the first time. I feel my kinship with Abraham when he lifted up his eyes and looked, and behold three men stood in front of him. My guest, like his, has paused on a journey. Do I really want to stop what I am doing and invite him to wash his feet and rest under the tree before he passes on? Geographically the journey is rarely impressive – an underground ride across town, a commuter train from New Jersey, or even a five-minute walk through the seminary close. The person standing at my office door is rarely dishevelled or dust-covered and would resist any attempt of mine to wash his feet. But spiritually he has come a great distance and is still far from home.

Like all of us, the person seeking spiritual direction is on a journey. Since the expulsion from Eden we have been a people on the move, despite attempts at self-delusion that we have somehow arrived. We follow in the footsteps of our peripatetic Lord, always on the way, our faces turned resolutely or reluctantly towards Jerusalem.

Mobility is our way of life. How many of us live within ten, even a hundred miles of our birthplace? And how many of us have any idea where we will die? Physically, our life is a journey. Spiritually, too, we are always on the way, *in via*, when we long to be *in patria*. We are travellers and we are homesick. We are travellers and we are weary.

It is a fact of life that travellers cannot survive in comfort without hospitality. However prudent their planning and abundant the supplies they carry, if the journey goes on long enough they will need the care of a host, someone who offers a temporary home as a place of rest and refreshment. Thus Abraham offered water for his angelic visitors to wash the dust from their feet, and fresh-baked bread and meat to ease their hunger. Thus too in America McDonald's golden arches and the familiar logo of the Holiday Inn beckon us off the motorway, promising dubious refreshment and homogenised rest. (The best surprise is no surprise, we are told. On the spiritual journey the reverse might well be true.) Even the most self-sufficient cannot escape the need for hospitality: modest family car and splendid mobile home alike turn into those discreetly labelled areas in national parks which invite them to empty their waste tanks before continuing the journey.

In the harsh circumstances of the desert or the frontier, hospitality offers more than comfort: it insures physical survival. Spiritually, too, we cannot make it through the desert or across the frontier alone. Like Blanche DuBois, in *A Streetcar Named Desire*, we must depend on the kindness of strangers. Unlike poor Blanche, by the grace of God those strangers upon whom we depend are not really strangers but our sisters and brothers in Christ. They are the hosts, the givers of hospitality who sustain us on the journey. They are our spiritual friends and directors.

'Host' is a word with many connotations, not all of them comfortable in the context of a discussion of spiritual direction. Talk shows have hosts – yet one would scarcely think of these hosts as bestowers of hospitality in the biblical sense. Air stewardesses used to be called hostesses, pretty young women who made sure that passengers were buckled into immobility before distributing drinks and little plastic containers of plastic food. A grim and sterile vision of hospitality!

Perhaps English speakers have devalued the words; certainly we lack the freshness and immediacy of the German *Gastgeber* – the guest-giver, the one who gives to guests – and *Gastfreundschaft* – guest-friendship, the special generous friendship shown by hosts to their guests.

The spiritual director is a host who gives, the bestower of guest-friendship. She is a host in the truest and deepest sense, reflecting the abundant hospitality shown by the host at the heavenly banquet.

Getting ready

Anyone who has ever given a dinner party or entertained weekend guests knows that hospitality is hard work, made even harder by the necessity that it should appear effortless. For Abraham it was easy: while he greeted his guests effusively, offering them the best that he had, his servant was butchering and dressing the calf and Sarah was scurrying around inside the tent making cakes.

For most of us in the West in the late twentieth-century, and certainly for those who practise spiritual direction as a ministry of hospitality, it is not so easy to delegate the real (that is, tedious and painstaking) work to others. The first step in being a good host, for dinner or for spiritual direction, is to get ready, to have the preparation done so that the scurrying may cease and the guest be greeted graciously.

Guests provide a helpful discipline. Left on our own, we can walk endlessly round disorder and uncleanness, vowing to do something about the state of our house some time, but not now. We may even come to love our muddle, to treasure it or at least to take it so for granted that it becomes a comfortable environment. But when an honoured guest is coming we carry out the rubbish, restore objects to their rightful places, and create an uncluttered, clean and welcoming space.

So it is also for spiritual directors. The first – and ongoing – task is one of housework, of creating our own inner order. We must know ourselves well, know our dark corners and our airless places, the spots where dust collects and mould begins to grow. It is not enough to push our rubbish into the cupboard and shut the door, nor to lower blinds and dim the lights so that the dirt doesn't show, although these are tempting tricks for harried caretakers of houses and of souls. No, we must clean our house, and then keep cleaning it so that we have a worthy place when we invite others to rest and refreshment.

Literal housecleaning is tiresome but straightforward work; scrubbing and polishing bear visible results, and we can check and admire our progress. Spiritual housecleaning is more subtle and something that spiritual directors cannot do unaided. Anyone presuming to undertake this ministry without the guidance of her own director is embarking on a dangerous path of self-deception, the spiritual equivalent of jamming all the junk into an out-of-the-way cupboard or shoving it down the cellar stairs to be dealt with later.

So the first step for any director is, with help, to become aware of himself, to know his areas of potential disproportion. Spiritually, the house must be kept in order, at least to the degree that it offers a wholesome, not a dangerous, environment to those who shelter there.

Some of my colleagues, operating from a psychotherapeutic model, would insist on a supervisor in addition to or perhaps instead of a director. There is much to be said for turning to a clinically competent, disinterested person to discuss the difficulties and concerns of one's work, for we need the resources of *all* the disciplines, but especially psychology. The peril lies in turning the directees – our guests, the recipients of our spiritual hospitality – into 'cases'. The director as bestower of hospitality is not a therapist (although she knows enough of human development and pathology to be able to make referrals when appropriate), and those to whom she offers care are not patients or clients, but journeyers who have turned aside and stopped for a moment.

Further, issues of confidentiality arise when the director works with a supervisor. The cure of souls is a tender work, and spiritual direction is closer to the confessional than to the physician's office. Both the priest and the physician are bound to guard the secrets revealed to them; but it is common, indeed necessary practice for the latter to consult others. Even when standards of confidentiality are impeccably observed, information about the patient is shared, in toto or in part, with a wide variety of persons beyond the primary physician – consultants, nurses, record-keepers and laboratory technicians, to name only a few.

But a directee is not a patient, and the material of direction does not constitute a 'case'. Rather, it is a gift received prayerfully and in trust, to be honoured and then to be let go. A wise priest friend told me early in my seminary training to learn to 'practise forgetting'; his was probably the most valuable advice I have received as a confessor or director.

But to return to the task of putting one's house in order: a psychotherapist may help, but one's own spiritual director (who may also serve as confessor) is essential. I must be willing to leave my own safe place and seek hospitality with another, to ask for help and let myself be guided. I must be willing to be the needy, vulnerable, weary traveller as well as the generous host. It is easier to be the host, as Abba James of the desert knew, when he said, 'It is better to receive hospitality than to offer it.'[1] Having a spiritual director keeps me honest. Having a spiritual director makes me aware of the corners of neglect and helps me keep the house at least reasonably tidy.

Spiritual directors need all the help they can get if they are to maintain themselves in a reasonable state of fitness. (No one expects perfection.) In addition to the very necessary director of one's own and the very helpful therapist, we all need spiritual friends to whom we can talk of our deepest concerns and who do not fear to speak the truth in love to us. The unofficial patron saint of spiritual directors, Aelred of Rievaulx, wrote in the twelfth century:

> . . . a man is to be compared to a beast if he has no one to rejoice with him in adversity, no one to whom to unburden his mind if any annoyance crosses his path or with whom to share some unusually sublime or illuminating inspiration. . . He is entirely alone who is without a friend. But what happiness, what security, what joy to have someone to whom you dare to speak on terms of equality as to another self; one to whom you can unblushingly make known what progress you have made in the spiritual life; one to whom you can entrust all the secrets of your heart and before whom you can place all your plans.[2]

I had never heard of Aelred when I first met my friend Janet, but later I recognised her in his words. She is English, a musician and a medievalist as well as a sensitive lay theologian. She gives me something which I cannot give myself. Except for her disapproval of my fondness for florid, late-nineteenth-century Russian piano music, she accepts and loves me as I am. I value her keen mind and uncompromising honesty; and although we have never analysed it, I know that our friendship is equally valuable to her. Distance keeps us from meeting oftener than about once a year, but each time there is a sense of homecoming and complete safety. There is no place for the trivial in our conversations nor any place for pious posturing. While we rarely pray together, our talk is always God-talk as

---

[1] Benedicta Ward, *The Desert Christian*, p. 104.
[2] Aelred of Rievaulx, *Spiritual Friendship* (UK distrib. Mowbray 1982; US Cistercian Publications 1977), pp. 71–2.

we 'speak in terms of equality as to another self'. I thank God for Janet, who helps to keep me real, honest and human. Those who turn to me for spiritual direction will never know their debt to her.

Then too there are those things which we can do for ourselves, which keep us ready to receive guests. I find the personal journal a great aid in self-awareness, for seeing what I am up to and what I am deviously concealing from myself. There are methods and disciplines of journal-keeping, some so formidable that they discourage all but the most zealous. A free-form, 'write when you need to' system works well for me. By keeping the journal in loose-leaf binders I am able to write on the typewriter or word processor and to include letters, poems, even articles that have become part of my story. Journal entries can be made at any time and any place, then carried home to be placed in the binder. Once I had decided that no one would read it, or if they did it wouldn't matter, since I would be dead, I have been able to write candidly. In the journal the writer can be as repetitive as he wishes; it's a great place to wrestle with angels and struggle with demons.

Retreat time also helps in maintaining a healthy perspective. A retreat is not synonymous with a holiday. There is an intentional austerity about a retreat. The radically simplified environment discourages inner clutter. In most religious houses there is 'nothing to do' – no games, no distractions, no loud noises, no TV, no busyness. Instead there is silence, simple food, adequate space and the security of being surrounded by a praying community. For those of us who get trapped in crowded schedules and who fall into the dangerous and sinful delusion that we, the administrative assistants of a well-meaning but inefficient Managing Director God, are really the ones who hold up the world, even a brief retreat is a powerful corrective. When we have slowed down we are able to look at ourselves and smile at our pitiful little constructs. Our humility is restored, that is, at least for a little while we are reminded of our true place in the order of things.

Spiritual directors, confessors, spiritual friends, and retreats – all quiet **spiritual** ways of keeping our house in order! Yet it is very easy to overlook the ordinary gifts of creation as aids to wholeness. Blessed are those who number babies and animals among their friends; in their embodied innocence such small creatures keep us simple. Blessed are those who find God or at least God's hand in the aesthetic; music, literature and art keep us joyful and proportionate. And blessed are those who enjoy good, hard work. There is nothing like sawing through a log or mowing a lawn, scrubbing a **very** dirty floor or kneading a loaf of bread to make us rejoice in our physicality and bring us close to the earth. A spiritual director who becomes too spiritual is more than a little frightening.

Sharing our space

What happens when we offer hospitality? Most simply, we invite someone into our space, a space that offers safety and shelter. The host's needs are put aside, as everything is focused on the comfort and refreshment of the guest. For a little while, at least, *mi casa es tu casa*, as the Spanish gracefully puts it. There are provisions for cleansing, food and rest. It is an occasion for storytelling where both laughter and tears are acceptable. After the interval of hospitality the guest moves on, perhaps with some provisions or a road map for the next stage of the journey.

At its simplest hospitality is a gift of space, both physical and spiritual. Like the gift of attentive listening, it is not to be valued lightly. This is brought home to me every day when I go to work. I live in New York, where the population density contributes to stress, even to the high degree of violence, and where one quickly becomes aware of the invisible lines that secure a modicum of psychological privacy. Thus one learns to avoid eye contact in the underground and to move briskly along crowded pavements, coming within millimetres of fellow pedestrians but without actually **touching** anyone. Space is treasured, space is guarded jealously. But as spiritual directors, we gladly share our space, the outer space of study or office and the inner space where God can be met. Unlike the New Yorker in the crowded street we do not fear being generous with our territory nor do we fear intimacy with another person. We offer the best that we have, the space which we have prepared.

Physical space is, in its way, as important as spiritual space. I find that I cannot work in my home: there is too much confusion of roles and personae. Even if family members and pets can be banished to other parts of the house, the impedimenta of daily living intrude themselves and make the space *too* personal, so that the direction session threatens to turn into a friendly chat. To meet in the directee's home is even less satisfactory, unless, of course, illness, age or frailty makes it difficult for them to come to us. Most public places are also difficult. I resist directees who wish to meet over lunch. How can you be prayerfully silent together when the waiter wants to tell you his name and recite the specials of the day? Even the quietest restaurant offers more distractions than I can cope with; the food itself is a distraction. (This is perhaps my own idiosyncrasy. I know other directors who find the intimacy of a shared meal a great help in their work, and I can envision a timid or resistant directee who would be more at ease in a semi-social setting, at least in the early stages of the relationship.)

Park benches are fine in good weather, and empty churches are a weekday resource. However a quiet room that is pleasant and uncluttered, humane but not overly personal, is preferable. Most of my work as a director is done in my office, a spacious and sunny room in an early-nineteenth-century building. (I am told that in gentler times it housed the seminary infirmarian, a connection which I find appropriate and comforting.) Before a meeting, I try at least to arrange the chaos on the desk into tidy piles and to push the word processor into its unobtrusive corner, minimal gestures of transforming 'business' space into 'holy' space.

When I first occupied this office I recoiled from the rug which delineated the 'conversation area' of the room. The chairs were all right, quite comfortable and not too bad to look at. But the rug! An unfortunate red plaid which had seen better days, it had visibly worn places and several tears on its edges. I vowed that it would have to go as soon as the budget would permit a replacement.

But now that rug has become an important part of the space. Again and again, in the silence at the beginning of a session, I would hear in my heart the words from Aelred's essay on spiritual friendship: 'Here we are, you and I, and I hope a third, Christ, is in our midst.' At some point, and I am not sure when, a place in the middle of that ghastly red plaid rug became holy. Even with the most lavish budget, I could never replace it now. Only last week a directee arrived from another city and said, 'You know, all the way on the train I kept seeing your rug.' I shared with her my quotation from Aelred. We laughed and we sighed and then agreed that the space between us was indeed holy, drawing us together rather than separating us.

The space offered for spiritual direction should be as welcoming as possible: icons, a plant or a few flowers, gentle light, a comfortable temperature and quiet are all helpful. More important, though, it should be a **safe** space, almost a sanctuary. On an immediate level it is safe because it is secure from interruptions. For people to walk through, enter the room or even knock on the door is more than a distraction; it is a violation. I always disconnect the telephone and hang a 'Do Not Disturb' sign on the door before we begin our work. Then we can pray together or sit in silence, weep or talk, and know that for a little while, for sixty minutes, there will be no intruders and no distractions. There is a sense of great spiritual space. Even though the time is limited (and I believe that this limitation should be observed, except in unusual circumstances), there is – paradoxically – the sense of all the time in the world. In the safe space that has been created the director can be totally committed, attentive only to the welfare of the guest.

The directee should feel unhurried. I find that people often arrive in a state of great distraction, perhaps anxious because the bus was slow or they couldn't find a parking place or because this meeting feels – somehow – like an appointment to talk with God, and they aren't sure how to begin the conversation. Perhaps this is why my first meeting with Thomas was decidedly uncomfortable: he is a physician, a third-year resident in an inner-city teaching hospital. His hours are long and his work demanding in wisdom and skill. He is surrounded by people in great pain, many of them facing death. God had got his attention, and going to church on Sunday wasn't enough to assuage his extreme spiritual discomfort. A mutual friend told Thomas about the Center, and he called for an appointment. In her enthusiasm the friend did us both an unwitting disservice by painting a glowing picture of spiritual direction in general and my gifts in particular. Thomas arrived, definitely wary of the highly-touted guru and not at all sure that candour in God-talk is a good idea. It took us several sessions of cautious testing (on his part) and determined ordinariness (on my part) before the space, physical and spiritual, felt truly welcoming to him.

Then, too, the director can unconsciously communicate his own hurriedness and distraction. Even though I try to allow a few minutes to collect myself between directees or to make the transition from educator-administrator to spiritual director, it doesn't always work. A seminarian arrives to wrestle with issues of vocation, or an incest survivor comes to talk about the difficulty of praying the Our Father while memories of an earthly father-rapist flood her mind – and I am caught up in syllabus preparation or altercations with the Business Office.

No matter how inviting the physical space might be, I have preparations to make before I can offer true hospitality.

Sharing the silence

It helps to begin with silence. If nothing else, the time with the directee is thereby set aside as prayerful time, not as a conference or a friendly chat. The length of the silence may vary. In the early stages of working together the directee may find it threatening, or at least unsettling, if the stillness goes on too long, but the quiet time can extend as trust grows. Emily and I once sat together for an hour in complete silence. We had worked together long enough to be comfortable with and trusting of one another. On that particular day she was exhausted from work and family pressures. I had invited her to break the silence when she was ready. Minutes passed, and the silence became deeper and deeper, serene but very alive. I felt present to her, but in no way anxious to 'do' anything for her. At the end of the hour we exchanged the peace, knowing that Aelred's Third had indeed been present in our midst.

The entry into silence need not be abrupt. Directees I have not seen for some time often arrive wanting a chat as much as spiritual direction. So we spend a minute or two catching up, perhaps getting a cup of tea or coffee, before we settle down to work. Then the silence helps define the borders, makes it clear what we are about.

During the initial moments of silence I try not to pay attention to the directee, but rather to get my own house in order. It helps to have an upright posture, hands open and relaxed, and breathing slowed. And then I pray – sometimes the Jesus Prayer, the prayer of the heart beloved in the Eastern Church: Lord Jesus Christ, Son of God, have mercy on me, a sinner. Sometimes they are fairly childish prayers of petition: Dear God, help me pay attention! Dear God, help me keep my mouth shut! Dear God, let me put myself out of the way! Dear God, let me be wholly present to this person, your child!

When I have quieted myself I can pay attention to the person sitting opposite me. I have read that physicians can make extensive and accurate diagnoses merely by shaking hands with the patient when he enters the consulting room. Silence shared with the directee is in some ways such a diagnostic instrument. Although we are not clinicians, it can tell us a great deal. With our eyes closed and our hearts centred in prayer we can pick up fear, anxiety, fatigue, rage, hope and yearning – the whole spectrum of human feeling that the Psalmist brings to God.

Sometimes, as with Emily, I ask the directee to end the silence when she is ready. Because people may feel put on the spot if they are asked to pray, I phrase this request in general terms: 'Let's be quiet together for a few minutes, and then you begin whenever you are ready.' I have learned to say this very clearly and with sufficient volume: prayerful silence is out of the question if either of us is not sure about the ground rules. For those who are still uneasy, somehow fearful of not saying 'the right things', the responsibility for beginning the conversation can be a burden. Then I end the silence with a prayer. Perhaps the Trisagion (Holy God, holy and mighty, holy immortal One, have mercy upon us), perhaps a simple 'Come, Lord Jesus', an invocation of the Holy Spirit, or just 'Amen'.

I have learned to trust the little prayers that come into my mind, having long ago given up the idea that there is one correct way of gathering the silence together and moving out of it. Now I catch myself wondering what will pop into my head. Not too long ago, I was surprised to hear inwardly a German table blessing that I had learned as a very small child. I resisted it, because we were not sitting at a table and it seemed so inappropriate. But it wouldn't go away, and so I broke the silence with a prayer which I have since come to use frequently: 'Come, Lord Jesus, and be our guest, and bless everything that you have given us.' Only upon reflection did I realise that it was a nearly perfect prayer of hospitality, a prayer about the mysterious reversal of host and guest which lies at the heart of spiritual direction.

A safe place

The space and time provided for the directee is not only safe because it is free from interruption. It is also safe because **anything** may be said without fear of destructive criticism or exposure. The confidentiality of the spiritual direction session is or should be as inviolable as that of the confessional. It is important to make this clear to the directee at the initial, exploratory meeting: that you will not discuss with others anything that has been said during your time together. This seal can lead to delicate, even humorous situations within a small community such as the seminary, where most of us wear several hats. The safest path for me has been the cultivation of amnesia, even about 'harmless' details, since it is difficult to remember where I first heard bits of news about jobs, pregnancies, crises and triumphs. Even in a larger context than the parish or a seminary, the spiritual direction community is a surprisingly small one. It is prudent to assume that **everyone** knows **everyone** and hence to resist the temptation to discuss one's work as a spiritual director in any but the most general terms.

For the same reason I am reluctant to maintain any kind of written records, although I know that some directors, including such prestigious ones as Martin Thornton,[3] advocate some form of record-keeping, as a reminder of relevant issues or as progress notes. In my view, however, this is one of the ways in which spiritual direction is distinguished from psychotherapy. We must have a discerning eye, but we are not diagnosticians in a clinical sense, for we risk diminishing our spiritual guests if we reduce them to symptoms and measurements. The person sitting opposite me is always a mystery. When I label, I limit.

People's secrets – the secrets of their lives and more especially the secrets of their souls – are precious. We live in a time when most of us can talk easily about sex, somewhat less comfortably about death (particularly our own), and only with the greatest difficulty about our relationship with God. To enquire how people pray is to ask THE intimate question. I still remember a time in a crowded bookshop when James, a young priest friend, said quite out of nowhere and in a voice that carried through the shop, 'You know, Margaret, you've never told me how you pray. What do you do, anyway?' I had a feeling of *déjà vu*, carried back to a time at the supermarket checkout when one of my children, in a clarion voice, asked, 'But how do the babies get **inside** in the first place?' To James, as with the child at the checkout, I hastily said, 'I'll tell you when we get outside.'

So prayer is an intensely private matter, and how we relate to God the most intimate question. Sometimes a long period of gentle waiting is necessary to establish the kind of trust that makes open, candid conversation possible. There is no hurry: true intimacy cannot be instant, and trust cannot be forced. Even when nothing seems to be happening, if we are prayerfully present to the directee, growth and movement *are* taking place.

The word 'pray', like other four-letter words, is heavily laden, so my approach is often circumspect. I might begin by

[3] Martin Thornton, *Spiritual Direction* (London, SPCK 1984; US, Cowley 1984), p. 127.

asking about the directee's daily rhythms – are there times when she can be alone and quiet? Are there places that feel especially 'safe' and close to God? A bit of self-disclosure might help. Carol was reluctant even to talk about prayer, anxious and apologetic that she wasn't praying 'enough' and that she certainly wasn't praying 'right'. One day I commented that, while reading the daily office sometimes seemed mechanical and dry, however commendable, God felt very close and prayer seemed very real in the stillness of the morning, before the alarm clock sounded. Carol then said: 'I pray the Connecticut Turnpike. I use the toll booths as markers, like the big beads on the rosary.' Her entire daily commute was a time of prayer, but she felt that it didn't count, that she should be doing something more spiritual, and that her ageing Toyota could not qualify as a holy space.

Beyond the predictable difficulty of talking about prayer in any circumstances, people come to us burdened by sin, real and imagined, and by shame. The person recovering from addiction needs to feel safe with us. The survivor of sexual abuse needs to know that no detail can shock or disgust us. The penitent needs to know that we hear but do not judge, that we stand ready to untangle the strands of sin and shame.

The space is safe because the directee is sure of the director's total acceptance. The director needs to be unshockable, which does not mean that sin is taken lightly or that the consequences of destructive or hurtful behaviour are glossed over. 'Oh well, never mind,' and 'You did WHAT?' are equally wicked and irresponsible reactions to the baring of a soul. The director who is convinced of God's love and mercy, even when the directee cannot accept such a premise, is able to accept any disclosure with equanimity and by her loving acceptance is able to model and reflect God's love, so yearned for by the directee who nevertheless despairs of his own worthiness to receive that love.

A good host gives the guest the sense that there is all the time in the world, even when they both know that time is a precious commodity. Some of the things I have already mentioned – silencing the telephone and guarding against knocks on the door, a few moments of centring before the directee arrives, and (most important) a time of prayerful silence before the true conversation begins – can be helpful.

But unless I am able to put **everything** aside I have failed in hospitality. Ordinary business can be banished with relative ease. It is more difficult to quiet deeper unrest, such as my own anger, fear or fatigue, all issues that have little to do with the person sitting opposite me. But if I am to do my work optimally they must be put aside, at least for the next hour. The gift of hospitality in this time is the gift of myself, which may not be much, but it is all that I have.

As someone who likes to talk and who enjoys human company, one of my hardest learnings in spiritual direction has been that less is frequently more. Unrestrained empathy can lead us to appropriation of the other person's experience, by posture and by facial expression if not by words. I guard myself (not always successfully) by two means. First, I use the Jesus Prayer, my 'egg-timer' prayer. When I feel myself crowding the directee emotionally or spiritually, I tell myself, 'Ten Jesus Prayers before you make any response!' Or when I become impatient that we seem to be getting nowhere, I promise myself, 'Five Jesus Prayers, and then you blow the whistle.' The results are amazing: that simple old prayer has held me back from foolishness and harm more often than I can tell. Secondly I pay attention to my hands. Grantly Dick Read, in his seminal book on natural childbirth, stressed the importance of a relaxed face: if the birthgiver was able to relax her facial muscles, she was able to relax totally. It's hard to watch my own face, but hands are another matter. So long as they are open and receptive in my lap or resting easily on the arms of my chair, I am able to convey a sense of leisure because I myself feel unhurried. So when I feel myself clenching, I hasten to unclench!

Drawing to a close

But hospitality must have a beginning and an end. Guests cease to be guests if they come to live with us. As director it is my responsibility to keep track of the time and to draw the meeting to a close at the proper moment. An hour is sufficient; after that the conversation tends to become repetitive or trivialised. (I make an exception for directees who travel from a considerable distance and whom I therefore see less frequently.) I am greatly helped by a small clock – actually a retired alarm clock – placed unobtrusively behind the visitor's chair. It enables me to note the passage of time without looking at my watch, which is an insulting gesture, to say the least, when the directee is deep in a description of his Dark Night of the Soul. About ten minutes before the time is up, I manage to interject, 'We'll have to stop in a few minutes.' These words almost always result in a sharp-ened focus, and the most important material of the session may be introduced at this point. It is tempting to extend the time when these 'doorknob manifestations' occur, but I try to resist the temptation. The directee needs to value our time together and make optimum use of it. So I usually say something like, 'That seems significant. Let's start with that next time.'

Listening to the story

'Important material' and 'significant' are judging, quantifying words, oriented towards production. If spiritual direction is hospitality, offering a place for rest and cleansing, the director's assessment of what is and is not valuable is at best skewed. Sometimes there is a great deal of refuse to be dumped (to use the caravan park image) or layers of rust to be scoured away (in the housewifely idiom of Catherine of Genoa). This calls for patience and openness on the part of the director. Storytelling needs to be unhurried and unharried. The listening host must be willing to let the structure unfold, to be sensitive to seeming repetitions – are they plodding in a circle or do they spiral? Are there gems hidden in the rubbish? Is the storyteller testing the reliability of the listener, denying herself the protagonist's role and centring everywhere but on herself? So Mildred wants to talk only about her husband's vocational crisis. What can she do to help him? And Jane wants to talk about her rector, for whom she functions as a kind of elder sister. How can he be protected from predatory churchwardens? And how can she help him learn to delegate responsibility?

Storytelling is a dance, a dialogue; and sometimes the listener-director must become active and help shape the story. So I might say to Mildred, 'This is your time, not David's. What about YOU?' And I must be prepared for the response, 'I want only what's best for him. I want to help him.' She is resistant. I cannot let her go on avoiding her own inner exploration, but neither can I become impatient with her. She must be willing to focus on herself, not because she fears my displeasure, but because she acknowledges her own worth. Or possibly because she knows that nothing in her *own* story, however shameful it might seem to her, is unsayable in the sheltering safety of the direction relationship. Jane is easier. A kind woman who loves to take care of people now that her children have left the nest, she needs only a gentle reminder that her rector can look after himself and that this is the time and place to look after Jane.

At least in the initial stages of the direction relationship, the story told may seem a secondary one, even (as with Mildred) a determined diversion. Understandably so, for this is a time of testing. Tony talks at length about his difficulties on the work scene, where the pressures of office politics make a mockery of his prayer life. What he says when we are together is all 'true', but I know that we are nowhere near the heart of the matter. We are spiralling ever closer, however. Not long ago he said to me, 'I think I trust you. There are more things I want to talk about some day.' I have no idea what these things might be and feel no particular curiosity about them. I know that they are deep spiritual concerns because Tony's life is Christ-centred; but beyond that I can only speculate. As host-director I respect his privacy and say only, 'I'm here when you want me. You'll know when the time is right.' Trust must be allowed to build. I discover that it forms in strata: just when I think we are hopelessly stuck in banalities or stranded on a plateau, there is a sudden new openness. Or, just when I think that we have 'arrived', we move to a new and deeper level. This discovery is a constant surprise, ever new.

But of course the greater surprise should be that anyone would trust me at all, would enter my tent and accept my hospitality! The fact of being entrusted with someone's soul, of being allowed to enter the story, however layered and convoluted it might be, is staggering. Fortunately there is yet another surprise in store for the spiritual director. Like Sarah baking the cakes or the unnamed servant dressing the calf, he is a necessary, but distinctly secondary figure in the offering of hospitality. Without warning, the role of host, of Guest Giver, is preempted! This should not be surprising, for the Gospel offers precedents: Jesus had a way of taking over at the dinner table. So too in the ministry of spiritual direction – when all is said and done the Holy Spirit is the true director. I find this reassuring when I am overcome by performance anxiety. Will I be wise? Will I be sufficiently holy, or at least look that way? Will I do even a half-way decent job? But if I am ready to relinquish my role to the true Host, the burden of responsibility drops away; and the space that I have prepared becomes gracious and holy.

When enough trust has developed so that the directee feels safe to discard diversions, the work of cleansing begins. Here the director's task is to discern between dirt and disorder, sin and shame. Most of us are well-meaning but cluttered, over-stimulated and pulled in a dozen directions at once. At the risk of romanticising, I suspect that the care of souls was easier in simpler times. I find that people sometimes come looking for a spiritual director because they are overwhelmed with GOOD things: challenging work, useful charitable activities, more books than they can read and more cultural events than they can absorb, more information than they can process, more paths of self-improvement than they can follow. Like over-indulged children they are inundated by good things; and they simultaneously yearn and fear to hear: 'One thing is needful.'

They come to a spiritual director because they want that one thing, even when they cannot articulate their need. They want help in clearing away the clutter, or at least in arranging it so that it becomes useful spiritual furniture rather than an impediment to wholeness.

Asking questions

Here the director can help by asking the right questions. Simple, direct questions that cut to the heart of the matter are part of the spiritual tradition. Jesus had a way of sweeping distractions out of the way with a trenchant question. To the blind beggar Bartimaeus he said: 'What do you want me to do for you?' To the disciples of John the Baptist, as they crept along behind him, attracted yet cautious: 'What do you seek?' To the disciples, despairing of having enough to feed the multitude: 'How many loaves have you? Go and see.' The four Gospels alone provide enough questions for spiritual directors to use in clearing away the clutter and helping the directee to articulate his yearning for God.

The question to Bartimaeus particularly is an invaluable aid to clarity and order. When the director asks it, he may meet with resistance, especially in women who have been early socialised to want nothing (at least overtly!) and to put their own needs aside in the service and care of others. This is a time to be gently persistent. 'What do you want me – as director – to do for you? What do you want him – Christ – to do for you?' To get at the answer is not unlike peeling an onion, having first persuaded the directee that it is 'all right' to want something, that a God who invites us to address him familiarly as Abba must expect childlike (if not childish) behaviour from us.

Directees who are the victims of niceness need to be reminded that such niceness, however painfully achieved and however

costly, is not one of the cardinal virtues. They are often surprised when I refer them to scriptural precedents for persistence, even nagging, in their prayers of petition. Even those who
claim moderate acquaintance with the Bible forget about the
Canaanite woman, who simply would not stop asking for Jesus'
help, even though he tried to dismiss her with an abruptness
that would earn a failure mark in pastoral 'presence':

> . . . she came and knelt before him, saying, 'Lord, help me.'
> And he answered, 'It is not fair to take the children's bread
> and throw it to the dogs.' She said, 'Yes, Lord, yet even
> the dogs eat the crumbs that fall from their masters' table.'
> Then Jesus answered her, 'O woman, great is your faith!
> Be it done for you as you desire.' And her daughter was
> healed instantly.[4]

This is a shocking story for those who believe that prayer must
be polite to the point of diffidence. Even more shocking are the
parables recorded by Luke, stories which seem to encourage
bad manners, even obnoxious behaviour in prayer. The man
who knocks persistently on his friend's door at midnight gets
what he wants by sheer tenacity: 'I tell you, though he [the
householder, trying to sleep] will not get up and give him anything because he is his friend, yet because of his importunity he
will rise and give him whatever he needs.'[5]

Directees who are fearful of somehow going too far and pro-
voking retribution from a God whose patience has been tested
to the breaking point can be helped by the humorous exagger-
ation in this parable as well as the ironic overstatement in the
story of the dishonest judge and the persistent widow. Like the
outcast Canaanite woman who refused to leave Jesus alone
until her daughter was healed, the widow does not let go lightly.
Finally the judge gives in: 'For a while he refused; but afterward
he said to himself, "Though I neither fear God nor regard man,
yet because this widow bothers me, I will vindicate her, or she
will wear me out by her continual coming." '[6]

To be able to say what one truly wants or where one is in pain
is a great step towards clarity, towards order in one's spiritual
household. People come to direction wanting and needing
many things but – unlike the troublesome widow – fearful of

[4] Matthew 15:25–28; also Mark 7:24–30.
[5] Luke 11:8–9.
[6] Luke 18:4–5.

'bothering' God and unaware of God's invitation to do just that! Further they come to us unsure of their priorities: in the material and emotional overabundance of our culture they have been stimulated to love and want many things. Augustine spoke wisely of the need to order our loves. Our directees come in the disarray of disordered loves, not knowing or perhaps only sensing their need to strip away the layers, to peel the spiritual onion and to be able to articulate what they really want: God. Augustine knew this when he wrote in his *Confessions*, 'Thou hast formed us for Thyself, and our hearts are restless till they find rest in Thee.'[7] Julian of Norwich knew it, when she prayed in the *Showings*, 'God, of your goodness, give me yourself, for you are enough for me, and I can ask nothing which is less which can pay you full worship. And if I ask anything which is less, always I am in want, but only in you do I have every-thing.'[8]

In a way, spiritual direction is a protracted discussion of the two great commandments:

> You shall love the Lord your God with all your heart, and with all your soul, and with all your mind. This is the great and first commandment. And a second is like it, You shall love your neighbour as yourself. On these two command-ments depend all the law and the prophets.[9]

When all the layers have been stripped away, God is what the directee wants. There may be other legitimate, laudable wants: physical and mental health, meaningful work, sound and stable relationships, to name just a few. And there may be other, less laudable loves and desires masked as pious yearnings: the desire to manipulate and control others, the avoidance of responsible engagement, spiritual posturing rooted in a cata-lytic mixture of pride and self-hatred – again to name but a few.

As the directee begins to create order out of the disorder of his loves, he begins to understand the breadth and depth of that love – love of God coming first, at the heart of the spiritual onion when the layers have been pulled away, but inextricably linked with love for all God's children. Including the directee himself.

---

[7] Augustine of Hippo, 'Confessions', in *Basic Writings of St Augustine*, ed. Whit-ney J. Oates (NY, Random House 1948), Vol. 1, p. 3.
[8] Julian of Norwich, *Showings* (NY, Paulist Press 1978), p. 184.
[9] Matthew 22:37–40.

Dealing with the rubbish

One of the great gifts of hospitality is the possibility for cleansing. When I was a student in Switzerland, decades ago, having a bath was not to be taken lightly: the water had to be heated, and sometimes the landlady charged extra for the fuel. In the house where I lived the privilege was free, but the bath was in an unheated, outdoor cellar. So when I visited friends who lived in a modern apartment with unlimited hot water, there was no question of how they might best entertain me – they retired early, leaving me to splash and soak. Now I enjoy repaying the debt of their hospitality: some of my favourite house guests in New York are young people who travel with backpacks and are used to the minimal comfort of hostels and dormitories. After I have fed them heartily I retire early, leaving them to enjoy the hot shower and the washing machine.

Order is not synonymous with cleanliness. People come to direction burdened with a sense of their own unworthiness, unloveliness and crushing shame, and their own sins. What a tangle! As the story is told, it is the director's task gently to pick apart the strands, never to minimise the directee's pain or responsibility for his own actions – and then to deal with the rubbish! There is the shame of the recovering addict, the lingering sense of uncleanness that haunts the incest survivor, the painful memory of an abortion, the anguish of broken relationships that can never be restored, the burden of trespasses long forgotten by all save the trespasser. There is great variety in the rubbish. It may contain hidden treasures and nearly always provides a fertile medium for growth. Even when it is unlovely and smells bad.

Those who come to spiritual direction burdened with their sinfulness come in need of cleansing and healing. Julian likens the errant soul to a headstrong toddler who must be free to run and explore her little world if she is to grow to maturity, but who inevitably falls, tearing her clothing and becoming hurt and dirty. This is a homely and engaging picture of the sinner, crying out – as Julian puts it – not to a God of punishment but to a loving mother Christ. The loving mother picks up the toddler, cleans and comforts it, then holds it close.

A good model for spiritual directors who deal with over-age errant toddlers! As we listen to the stories of our guests, again and again we hear them say the twentieth-century equivalent of Julian's words: 'My kind mother, my gracious mother, my beloved mother, have mercy on me. I have made myself filthy and unlike you, and I may not and cannot make it right without your grace and help.[10]

I am struck by the overlap of spiritual direction and sacramental confession. It is essential that the story be told candidly, that sins and shortcomings be named, that the directee see himself clearly. St Anthony in the desert knew the importance of recognising and naming the demons. Exposure is salutary. My grandmother, living before the time of antibiotics and practising the folk medicine inherited from her rural foremothers, knew that healing was promoted by cleansing, then by exposure to light and air.

So as spiritual directors, whether we are lay or ordained, we are purveyors of light and air: we hear confessions. We hear stories of hurt received and hurt inflicted, of shabbiness and coldness of heart, of myriad little murders. Some of our directees might shrink if we began the session by inviting them to make a formal sacramental confession, but if we let them know that we sense their burden and gently invite them merely to speak of it, the sense of relief is almost palpable. Others who are at ease with the sacrament of reconciliation may use spiritual direction as a means of preparing for confession; or, if the director is also the confessor, regular celebration of the sacrament can be woven into the fabric of the relationship.

In the *Parzival* of Wolfram von Eschenbach, the foolish knight has travelled and quested for years, unwittingly leaving hurt and destruction in his wake – he has left his mother to die of loneliness and a broken heart, he has killed his (unrecognised) cousin and then despoiled the corpse, he has brought degradation and suffering to a married woman whose husband did not understand his clumsy and asexual embraces of her. Most seriously, he has let social convention stand in the way of true compassion, for when he saw the excruciating suffering of the Grail King, his mistaken understanding of chivalric behaviour prevented his asking the saving question: 'What's wrong? What hurts?'

On Good Friday, chance or grace brings him to the hermit Trevrizent. What occurs between them is a model of hospitality and a model of spiritual direction, particularly in its purgative and healing aspects. The old man knows that the youth is burdened with anger and guilt, that he lacks self-understanding,

[10] *Showings*, p. 301.

and that he is spiritually as well as physically lost in a trackless wasteland. But like a good director, he is patient; he is able to sit quietly until the right moment has come. (*Pace* T. S. Eliot, who wisely tells us in *Four Quartets* that humankind is able to bear just so much reality.) He helps Parzival feed and stable his (stolen) horse; he invites the young man to warm himself by the meagre fire; he shares his simple food with him. Then, when Parzival can no longer contain himself – physical and spiritual comfort here seems inversely related; or perhaps, as a wise host, Trevrizent knows the importance of caring for the body as well as and perhaps before the soul – he tells his story. Or rather, he makes his confession, for his story is one long account of wandering far from God.

Trevrizent hears it gravely, without minimising or dismissing anything. Then, in a kind of absolution, he tells Parzival: 'Give your sins to me. In the sight of God, I am guaranty for your atonement.'[11] Sitting in his cold cave in a Germanic forest he is a northern echo of Abba Lot, austere father of the Egyptian desert, who said to his troubled penitent, 'Confess it [your sin] to me, and I will carry it.'[12]

This is perhaps the ultimate act of hospitality, epitomising the generous mutuality of the direction relationship. There is hierarchy, but it is dismissed. Like Abba Bessarion, the director knows that he too is a sinner: 'A brother who had sinned was turned out of his church by the priest; Abba Bessarion got up and went to him, saying, "I, too, am a sinner." '[13] Director and directee are united in the glory and sinfulness of their humanity; they are part of the same family. This is strikingly demonstrated in the courtly epic, where Trevrizent is revealed as Parzival's uncle; in the world of the Grail – and in this world too – **everyone** is related.

When we listen compassionately with 'the mind in the heart', as Theophan the Recluse puts it, we cannot help taking others' sins upon ourselves. After a day of listening I often feel heavy and tired, with queasy stomach and aching head. It helped me to understand my somatic reactions when I remembered novelist-theologian Charles Williams and his theory of 'exchange' and 'substituted love'. He takes very seriously the exhortation in Paul's letter to the Galatians that we 'bear one another's

[11] Wolfram von Eschenbach, *Parzival*, tr. Helen M. Mustard and Charles E. Passage (NY, Vintage 1961), p. 268.
[12] Benedicta Ward, p. 122.
[13] Ibid.

burdens and so fulfil the law of Christ'[14] and might have been writing for uneasy spiritual directors when he says:

> St Paul's injunction is to such acts as 'fulfil the law of Christ', that is, to acts of substitution. To take over the grief or the fear or the anxiety of another is precisely that; and precisely that is less practised than praised.[15]

Williams notes that this exchange requires 'practice and intelligence'. Like the spiritual direction relationship in general, it is contractual:

> The one who gives has to remember that he has parted with his burden, that it is being carried by another, that his part is to believe that and be at peace. . . The one who takes has to set himself – mind and emotion and sensation – to the burden, to know it, imagine it, receive it – and sometimes not to be taken aback by the swiftness of the divine grace and the lightness of the burden.[16]

I am rarely taken aback by the swiftness of the divine grace and the lightness of the burden, but I am working on it. There is a cheapness and spiritual dishonesty in opening oneself to another's story while keeping one's fingers crossed – 'I'll let it touch me, even touch me deeply, but not for long.' On the other hand I accept the burden, not to hoard and cherish it as mine but rather to pass it on immediately. As Williams observes, 'the carrying of the cross may be light because it is not to the crucifixion'.[17] I am still learning my obligations in the contract, and perhaps I am slow to let go. Yet I cannot believe that it is so effortless as Williams suggests. Unless I experience some heaviness, how do I know that I have accepted a burden?

This is a tricky business. We must avoid over-identification, whereby we appropriate the experience of the other and somehow make ourselves chief actors in the drama. And we must avoid the danger of becoming spiritual voyeurs, scarcely a problem if we remember who we are and our true place in the order of things. But we cannot help taking on some pain and darkness, if we sit compassionately with the directee like Trevrizent with Parzival in the cave. There we are open; we are

---

[14] Galatians 6:2.
[15] Charles Williams, *He Came down from Heaven* (UK distrib. Paternoster Press; US Eerdmans 1984), p. 123.
[16] Ibid., p. 125.
[17] Ibid., p. 124.

present emotionally as well as intellectually, and we will inevitably share some of the wounds and filth – or at least, scratches and dust.

In our culture it often seems a mark of professionalism to be impervious to others' pain. Sometimes this is a good thing: I would prefer that my surgeon operated with eyes not blurred with tears! But in many areas we have gone too far, and, along with their own woundedness, our healers deny the reality of others' suffering. But, thank God, spiritual directors are not professionals but amateurs who aspire to reflect Christ's love. So we take sin and pain upon ourselves, not in grandiose self-promotion, but because the assumption of such a burden is one of the risks of spiritual hospitality.

Yet we don't have to keep that burden, dragging ever-heavier loads of pain and sin until those close to us shrink back in the presence of our holy masochism. We can let it go in our prayers, in our prayers for ourselves and for our directees. We can let it go in holy forgetting, remembering that God was managing quite nicely before we joined the firm and will continue to cope after we have returned to dust. We can let it go by all our devices for refreshment and self-restoration. **But first of all, we must let ourselves be touched**. Trevrizent's hospitality was not cheap, even though the accommodations were minimal and the food a handful of herbs.

As spiritual directors we have the authority to assure our directees of God's love and forgiveness, and those of us who are ordained can declare absolution. While I like to know what I'm doing and therefore prefer to keep spiritual direction and sacramental confession distinct and clearly labelled, there are times when it is appropriate to say, 'What you have just told me is a confession. I am convinced that you are deeply sorry for these things in your past, indeed contrite. So I would like to offer you absolution.' For those to whom this is alien, even a little frightening, some brief teaching is in order. Then, as we end our meeting with absolution and a blessing, I can almost feel the heaviness drop from the directee.

Sometimes it is more appropriate to suggest that the directee considers making a formal confession in the near future. On one occasion, when I was conducting a retreat, a woman sought me out for a private conversation and told me about her abortion, performed decades ago when she was very young. At the time it had seemed her only course, but she had never ceased to mourn secretly for her unborn child. She seemed surprised when I spoke of her obvious love for her baby; she had seen only her guilt, not the love entangled and enmeshed in it. She was not accustomed to making her confession, so I suggested she looked at the rite of reconciliation in the American Book of Common Prayer, particularly at the second form. Then, if it seemed right to her, we would celebrate the sacrament together that evening. We did, tearfully. I have never felt so sure that there was indeed rejoicing in heaven as we embraced and I told her to go in peace, that the Lord had put away all her sins.

Lay directors and those from traditions where the sacrament of reconciliation is not celebrated need to remember that all baptised persons can declare God's forgiveness to those who are truly contrite. In my hospital ministry, before I was ordained, I once visited a woman scheduled for major surgery the next morning. She told me that she was a Roman Catholic, but that she had not made her confession for a very long time. When I offered to call the Roman Catholic chaplain she responded with mingled panic and despair, 'No, no, it's too late!' We sat together for a while – at her invitation, I was breaking hospital rules by sitting beside her on the bed – and then I said, 'But you want to tell God that you are sorry?' She didn't say anything, but fell into my arms and wept. I knew then that I had witnessed the gift of tears! After a moment I assured her of God's forgiveness. We exchanged the peace, and I wished her a good night. (She survived her open heart surgery. It is my prayer that she has found her way back to the Church.)

Sharing the story

Not all the storytelling of spiritual direction is confession, or at least not confession in the narrow sense. But for me, spiritual direction is **always** storytelling. I don't mean that we move doggedly through the directee's life, year by year and decade by decade. The story moves around in time, gliding or leaping from present to past, from present to future. Without the story, there is no flesh, no blood, no specificity. But I find that it doesn't matter where we begin. It is always a story of a journey, always a story about relationship with God – whether the directee is fleeing the Hound of Heaven, or is lost or yearning or living among the swine and eating their husks.

We all have a story. We **are** a story. The director's task is to help connect the individual's story to **the** story and thereby help the directee to recognise and claim his identity in Christ.

Together director and directee try to discern the action of the Holy Spirit in the latter's life. There is a God-component in all human experience, even when the directee's life seems pain-filled and remote from God. A sense of God's absence or remorse at one's own inattentiveness to God's presence can be a fruitful place for beginning direction. However the narration is structured, it eventually includes fragments of the story from the past, the present and the future.

I am uncomfortable with directees who insist they were always fully grown, conscious adults or with those who insist that the past doesn't matter. Our wounds do not necessarily disable us; indeed they can be transformed into a source of strength. For good or ill, they contribute to our texture. For example, the distinctive spirituality of adult children of alcoholic parents has been noted in numerous books and articles. These people often have a highly developed sense of responsibility; they are good at caring for others, cautious about too much intimacy, and doubtful of their own worth. Trust comes for them slowly in the direction relationship. Incest survivors are another group with a particular spirituality. They may be burdened with shame or struggling against their suppressed rage (at the parent who violated them and – often at a deep and hidden level – the 'out-to-lunch' God who let the abuse take place). Paternal imagery for God may be profoundly disturbing. Typically, they are quick to blame themselves for the pain and confusion in their lives.

Even when the directee's earlier life has not been marked by extraordinary suffering and pathology, the story of his beginnings is important if we are to have a sense of the whole person. To give only a few examples: birth order, ethnicity and remembered familial warmth (or lack thereof) all contribute colour and form to the picture. I always like to explore the directee's earliest awareness of God, which is often quite distinct from his family's degree of religious observance. For many people spiritual direction can be the first opportunity to articulate this experience.

As for the story of the present, it is absurd to talk about 'prayer' as an abstraction. There must always be a connection with the directee's 'real' life. This does not mean that there is no talk of prayer as such. People come to us seeking practical help in finding the rhythms and forms of prayer which are most fruitful for them. But I am nervous of a disembodied directee who wants to talk **only** of prayer. In such circumstances I feel free to ask questions: tell me about your work, your family, your friends, your health. Where is your Christian community? What do you do for fun? Again and again I discover that deep concerns have been pushed aside or submerged, as not being sufficiently 'spiritual' to discuss in this setting. A deteriorating marriage, an adolescent son caught in addiction, or daily work that deadens the soul are all spiritual issues and, as such, a crucial part of the story.

And the story must reach into the future. Spiritual direction is about hope. There is always a next step. One of my most helpful spiritual mentors in helping directees discern this next step is Mr Dick, Aunt Betsey's eccentric lodger in Charles Dickens' *David Copperfield*. Nowadays he would be classified as 'developmentally impaired', but Dickens presents him as childlike, loving and firmly grounded in reality. Repeatedly Aunt Betsey turns to him for counsel in complicated situations; his advice is always compassionate and eminently practical, going right to the heart of the matter. Confronted with a dirty, hungry, exhausted runaway child, he is cheerfully unaware of legal and familial complexities.

> 'Well, then,' returned my aunt . . . 'how can you pretend to be wool-gathering, Dick, when you are as sharp as a surgeon's lancet? Now here you see young David Copperfield, and the question I put to you is, what shall I do with him?'
>
> 'What shall you do with him?' said Mr Dick feebly, scratching his head. 'Oh! do with him?'
>
> 'Yes,' said my aunt with a grave look, and her forefinger held up. 'Come! I want some very sound advice.'
>
> 'Why, if I was you,' said Mr Dick, considering, and looking vacantly at me, 'I should – ' The contemplation of me seemed to inspire him with a sudden idea, and he added briskly, 'I should wash him!'[18]

Similarly, when the child becomes a permanent member of this unlikely household, Mr Dick does not borrow trouble by speculating about possible courses of action far in the future, but suggests with great practicality, 'Have him measured for a suit of clothes directly.'[19] (At this point David has nothing to wear but clothes borrowed from Mr Dick; they engulf his small

[18] Charles Dickens, *David Copperfield*, 1849.
[19] Ibid.

frame.) Our directees rarely need to be provided with literal scrubbing or garments, but their next steps, to be taken in hope, are often as small and simple as those offered by Mr Dick. The journey is not to be completed in a day, and the path leading to its end is twisted and invisible. But we can help them see the next small, often deceptively simple steps.

If spiritual direction is about hope, it is also about death. When I left secular teaching to pursue ordination to the priesthood, I felt called to work with the dying. Practical experience in the hospital and with the frail aged in a nursing home confirmed my gifts in this ministry. While it was emotionally and spiritually taxing, it was also fulfilling beyond all my expectations. It must be a sign of God's gracious (and ironic) humour that I no longer walk dark and empty corridors in the middle of the night or watch physical strength diminish and once-clear minds grow dim with the ravages of age. At first I was disappointed to exchange work at life's threshold for this quiet, well-groomed business of sitting and listening. But then I realised: I am still working with the dying! It is no longer fashionable to talk about 'a good death' and certainly not about preparing for a good death, yet that is what spiritual direction is all about. The journey does have an end, and our physical death is one of its markers. Even when it is not clearly articulated, people come to spiritual direction grappling with questions of their own mortality. We can help in this as we explore the story of the future.

Self-disclosure

Storytelling, as I have noted, is not a solitary activity. Like the tango, it takes two. The director is primarily a listener, but as such, a participant in her own right. Sometimes her participation appears passive, consisting chiefly of keeping quiet and staying out of the way, attentive but not overpowering. (Directors need to practise custody of the eyes – prolonged eye contact, however lovingly intended, can be as intrusive as a clumsy remark.) But sometimes the director's participation is more active, for she does not fear the self-revelation that comes from joining the conversation. It may be no more than acknowledging one's own difficulties in faithfulness at prayer or the all-too-human flaw of unreal expectations, spiritual or otherwise. Directees tend to set extremely high standards for themselves and expect that, in their new state of spiritual self-awareness, they will not become impatient or succumb to petty maliciousness. The director's shared humanity can be a valuable corrective.

This willingness towards self-disclosure is one of the primary distinctions between spiritual direction and psychotherapy. The mutuality of the former is an essential characteristic of the relationship. The director should always be aware that she too is a traveller, not an authority or a guru. Thoughtful self-disclosure is one way of remaining grounded and human. This must be done intentionally and judiciously, or else the direction session will degenerate into a cosy chat. So I ask myself: 'Why am I doing this? Will it help the directee? Or will my self-revelation be harmful, appropriating time, attention and energy that rightly belong to the person sitting opposite me?'

I try to avoid the exchange of friendly family anecdotes. Most of my directees know I am married and that I have brought up children; but specifics about my family are usually irrelevant. They all know that I am a priest. They can judge my age approximately by looking at me or precisely by consulting the Clerical Directory. Occasionally they will want to know more, and almost always for good reason: how did I get to where I am – externally, as director of the Center for Christian Spirituality and part of a seminary faculty, and on a deeper level as an amateur amma in the desert of New York? There are points at which hearing some of the director's story is an encouragement, not because the director has 'arrived' and hence merits emulation, but rather as a reassurance and reminder that we are travelling the same road.

So in initial meetings I make it a practice to ask if there is anything about me the directee would like to know. The most common questions at this point are, 'What brought you here? How did you start doing this work?' As the relationship develops and a moderate level of mutual comfort has been established, the directee is usually able to take the initiative and ask questions without my specific invitation. Now the most common questions are, 'Did you ever feel this way? Did this ever happen to you?' Tacitly, I have given permission to be challenged and probed to the degree that such sharing of experience is helpful to the directee. This is a delicate and dangerous business, for I can use the directee to feed my ego. By unspoken and even unconscious agreement, we can shift the focus of the storytelling to make me the main character. For example, I have to be specially careful with Jo, who is eager to attribute to me wisdom and compassion beyond my most extravagant dreams. It feels good! But I know that I am in danger of seduction, however loving and unwitting its intent; and so I resist her invitation to talk very much about myself.

However I join in the storytelling, whether by the directee's invitation or my own intuition, our sense of solidarity is increased. We are united in our sinfulness, our baptism and the commonalities of our journeys. I need not say much, just a few words to help make the connections. Thus to Penny, mother of a troubled and troubling teenager, I remarked: 'Being a mother can be heartbreaking work. Everyone who's been there has at least a little idea of what you're going through.' Penny didn't need to hear details of my life as mother of (now happily grown-up) adolescents, but it was liberating and helpful for her to know that we shared this particular kind of experience.

Careful self-revelation by the director is also helpful in dealing with projection and transference. Like all human beings, directees see that they want to see and hence attribute to us impossible degress of holiness and wisdom. Like Jo, who would rather hear about me than talk about herself, they are unwilling to let us be ourselves, that is, mere humans capable of sin and shabbiness. Instead they are willing, indeed eager, to elevate us to great heights of wisdom and sanctity. By our responses we can buy into this spiritual inflation, or we can apply a needed corrective. Particularly in the early stages of the relationship and particularly with those to whom the whole idea of spiritual direction is new, we run the risk of being put on a pedestal. We can defuse this by what we choose to reveal about ourselves – our own falling short in prayer; our tendency towards sloth, impatience or greed; our times of aridity. By no means do we turn the relationship round and overwhelm the directee with our own shortcomings. Rather, carefully and lightly, we try to communicate that the spiritual director has neither magic powers nor a direct line to God's ear, but is only a fellow traveller – at a different place on the road perhaps, but a fallible and ordinary traveller none the less.

We reveal ourselves in more than our words. Anyone coming into my office knows that I love icon reproductions, that my bookshelf is eclectic, that I support the ordination of women to the episcopate (a regal purple tea-cloth, given to me by English friends and tacked on the inside of the door, proclaims this), and that I like rocks from my beloved Virginia river and fresh flowers from the corner greengrocer. All this says more about me than framed certificates and diplomas, but – I hope – does not say so much that the directee is flooded.

We reveal ourselves also in what we wear. This is more of an issue for directors who are clergy or members of religious orders, for a black shirt and stiff white collar or a habit carries a powerful message of authority and hierarchy. Sometimes this is helpful: directees want to be sure that they are entrusting themselves to someone who is competent. Clerical garb offers some (not necessarily infallible) assurance of this. Further it depersonalises the situation, in that we present ourselves as 'priest' or 'religious' and not as 'man' or 'woman'. This can backfire, however, when – as frequently and quite healthily occurs – the directee confuses intimacy with God with human intimacy. Add to this romanticised projections about God-people in costume, and clerical or religious dress becomes an impediment.

So I am intentional in what I wear when I do spiritual direction. Some people are most comfortable talking with a clearly labelled priest, particularly when they are still testing the waters of our relationship or when they are dealing with painful or shame-filled material. Others are over-impressed by externals and have difficulty getting down to reality. If the director is in full costume, they seem to think, it is proper to talk only about prayer in the narrowest sense and to avoid any faintly 'improper' language or emotions. It is understandable that they may fail to see the human being beneath the plastic collar, but inexcusable if I join them in their fantasies. With such directees it helps to turn up at least part of the time in an unremarkable dress or suit; I haven't gone as far as jeans and a sweat-shirt, but I can imagine situations in which such informality would be liberating.

However it is achieved – by the director's self-revelation in word, dress or environment – the relationship is one of mutuality. She is not an impassive receiver of the story; rather, energy flows back and forth between the partners in the conversation. I am constantly surprised at how much shared laughter there is in spiritual direction. At first this felt inappropriate, and I was sure that I was doing something wrong. After all, spiritual direction is a serious business, and surely laughter has no place in it. But again and again, I find myself laughing **with** directees, never **at** them. What a pity there is no reference in the gospels to our Lord's laughter! Gentle, non-intrusive humour has a way of restoring perspective, or reducing our inflated selves to manageable proportions. Laughter makes and keeps us childlike.

And we also share tears. I do not cry easily, especially in the presence of others; but there are times in spiritual direction when words are quite out of place and, to my initial dismay, I feel tears flooding my eyes. This happened in my work with Linda, a survivor of years of incestuous abuse. I was with her as her story unfolded; and more than once as she shared the details of pain and degradation beyond imagination I was without words. There **were** no words which were not cheap, which did not somehow dishonour her experience. And more than once I felt my eyes fill and my cheeks grow wet. For a while I tried to deal with my tears surreptitiously; after all, it didn't seem professional behaviour! So I would prop my chin on my hand, in a posture of intense listening and make what I thought were unobtrusive swipes at the tears. Years have passed, and now Linda has reached a place of grace and hope. Not long ago she said to me, 'I can't tell you how much it meant to me the times you cried with me.' So much for my studiedly casual whisking away of my tears! By no means do I recommend weeping as a device, nor do I suggest that directors train themselves to cry on cue. But the importance of shared emotion, of empathy and compassion cannot be underestimated.

Angels unawares

Traditionally spiritual direction is a covenanted relationship between two persons. In practice it presupposes a degree of spiritual sophistication and a certain fluency of spiritual vocabulary. The picture comes to mind of two well-dressed people sitting in a tastefully furnished room, perhaps with a crucifix or an icon or two, talking about the life of prayer. Is this a real Dark Night of the Soul, or merely a Dark Night of the Senses? What shall I do, now that I am experiencing aridity in saying the office? Am I temperamentally suited for apophatic prayer, or should I be content with my present kataphatic practices? And is it true that imageless centring prayer is better than my sleeves-rolled-up conversations with God while I stand at the kitchen sink?

The ministry of spiritual direction stands always in the suspicion of élitism – spiritual élitism as well as educational and economic élitism. After all, one needs a certain amount of leisure to engage in introspection: when physical survival is at stake there is little time for picking at spiritual scabs. While I would in no way denigrate traditional spiritual direction – after all, it is my chief work – I am aware that we are in danger of isolating ourselves, of limiting our ministry to those like ourselves in carefully controlled situations. What a perversion if we come to see spiritual direction as a luxury for the educated, leisured, and affluent!

The author of the Letter to the Hebrews reminds us that we never know who may turn up on our doorstep, that – like Abraham – we should show ready hospitality because we may be entertaining angels unawares. Certainly, when we limit our work to formal situations, to churches, studies and offices, we risk neglecting those angels.

It has been my experience that much spiritual direction goes unnamed. Ministry to the sick and the dying is or should be spiritual direction. All too often we see it as 'friendly visiting' with the aim of 'cheering up' the sufferer – and giving our own ego a boost at the same time. (Once when I returned from a night of vigil with the family of a dying man a friend unwittingly remarked, 'What wonderful work you do! It must feel so good to go round cheering people up.') Even in apparently chance encounters there is the opportunity to offer the shelter of a safe and holy space.

The safe and holy space may be at a bedside, in the stark and sterile waiting-rooms of hospital corridors, or in the close quarters of an aeroplane. On a flight from Dallas to New York I sat next to a man who hadn't seen a woman in a clerical collar before. We chatted in a superficial way about changing times, his experience of the Church as a boy – he acknowledged that he didn't get to church much, any more – and then he said, 'Margaret, my father is dying. I've just come from visiting him. I have to get back home, but I know I won't see him again. Do you mind if we turn off the reading lights and just sit together quietly for a while?' I asked his father's Christian name so that I could pray for him. Then we sat together in the silent darkness for over an hour until the plane touched down at Kennedy Airport. My younger friend – I have forgotten his name and his face but I shall never forget him – reached for his luggage in the overhead rack and said, 'Thanks. That helped a lot.'

It was a time of spiritual direction, although I'm not altogether sure who was directing whom. It was a time when I offered hospitality, a safe space, although I am ashamed to acknowledge that my guest had to ask to be admitted, that I was prepared to go on reading my book – not closing him out but certainly not inviting him in.

Extension of the ministry of spiritual direction to those we have relegated to society's margins is an exciting prospect, but scarcely a new phenomenon. The story of Jesus' encounter with the Samaritan woman reminds us that we have a model for such a departure. As a woman and a Samaritan she was an outsider, invisible at best and despised at worst. Yet he accepted her hospitality by asking for a drink of water, then reversed the roles of host and guest as he offered her spiritual hospitality, indeed spiritual direction.[20]

All too often our ministry to those whom we have marginal-ised, pushed to the edge of our consciousness or even rendered invisible, consists of doing something 'for' them – the brisk and falsely cheery visit to the very ill or frail aged, the food pantry or shelter programme for the hungry and homeless, the carefully orchestrated and impersonal entertainment or religious service offered in a nursing home. Corporal works of mercy are of course our obligation; and while it is altogether possible to com-bine care of the physical person with care for his soul, it is also possible to hide behind good works and thereby avoid the cost of shared vulnerability and true attentiveness.

When I began work at a large Manhattan nursing home, the staff member showing me round the building wanted to whisk me past the second and third floors. 'These are the skilled nurs-ing floors,' he explained. 'Most of the people here are in terrible shape – can't talk, awfully confused, don't understand much of anything. You won't be here much. Let's go upstairs so that I can introduce you to some of our more alert residents.' As it turned out I spent at least half my time with the invisible people on the second and third floors. And there I learned about enter-taining angels unawares. It was a ministry of listening, not talk-ing, listening very hard in conversations that seemed to ramble endlessly, yet contained rich nuggets of truth and human feel-ing. Sometimes it was a ministry of touch and presence. Always it was a ministry of surprise, surprise at the gift of hospitality that I could bring in my non-judgmental, agenda-less listening. People were able to talk about death without a falsely cheery reassurance that they needn't and shouldn't think about such things. (Meaning, of course, 'You make me uncomfortable when you talk about something deep and real, especially some-

[20] John 4:7–26.

thing so deep and real as death.') They were able to go back in memories, find cause for celebration in recollection of times when their bodies were joyful instruments, not painful prisons. (Jeanne, confined to a wheelchair and not quite sure what decade it was – let alone what day, month and year – celebrated all creation when she talked about taking off her shoes and dancing barefoot for Isadora Duncan.)

My ministry on the skilled nursing floors was hardly spiritual direction in the classic sense, yet questions of deep meaning were addressed, pain and fear acknowledged, and the presence of the Holy Spirit always invoked (at least in my silent prayer upon entering the floor).

We can bring a rich gift of spiritual hospitality to all sorts and conditions of people – in our daily work, in chance encounters, in ministry undertaken to alleviate the physical suffering of the twentieth-century equivalents of the Samaritan woman. To let them into our space, our spiritual space if not our kitchens and living-rooms, is a costly ministry, for they will cease to be invisible. We will see their full humanity, and we will see Christ in them.

2

THE SPIRITUAL DIRECTOR
AS TEACHER

And as he was setting out on his journey, a man ran up and knelt before him, and asked him, 'Good Teacher, what must I do to inherit eternal life?' And Jesus said to him, 'Why do you call me good? No one is good but God alone. You know the commandments: "Do not kill, Do not commit adultery, Do not steal, Do not bear false witness, Do not defraud, Honour your father and mother."' And he said to him, 'Teacher, all these I have observed from my youth.' And Jesus looking upon him loved him, and said to him, 'You lack one thing; go, sell what you have, and give to the poor, and you will have treasure in heaven; and come, follow me.' At that saying his countenance fell, and he went away sorrowful; for he had great possessions. (Mark 10:17–22)

Amma Theodora said that 'a teacher ought to be a stranger to the desire for domination, vain-glory, and pride; one should not be able to fool him by flattery, nor blind him by gifts, nor conquer him by the stomach, nor dominate him by anger; but he should be patient, gentle, and humble as far as possible; he must be tested and without partisanship, full of concern, and a lover of souls'. (Benedicta Ward, The Desert Christian, *pp. 83–4)*

The purpose of education is to show a person how to define himself authentically and spontaneously in relation to his world – not to impose a prefabricated definition of the world, still less an arbitrary definition of the individual himself. (Thomas Merton, Love and Living, *p. 3)*[1]

EVERY NOW and then I ride with that vanishing breed of New Yorker philosopher-cabdriver, streetwise men with gifts of discernment. And I hear, 'You're a teacher, right, lady?' And I have to say, 'Yes, I am,' while I wonder what

---

[1] London, Sheldon Press 1979; New York, Farrar, Straus & Giroux 1979.

gave me away. I am lots of other things – priest, wife, mother, administrator, unauthorised medical practitioner, scrubber of floors and washer of clothes. But my teacher identity is one that has been with me for nearly as long as I can remember, and it is a true identity, inextricably linked with my priestly one.

I was about six when the pedagogical urge came over me. I had just learned to read and couldn't wait to impart my new-found skills to my best friend, Peggy, who was two years younger and considerably smaller than I. So we 'played school' interminably. In those days I was a fairly authoritarian teacher; but otherwise things haven't changed much. The excitement of sharing what has been learned, of mutual exploration and discovery, has remained with me. While most of my professional life has been spent in the college classroom, my experience has been varied – I have been teacher of English to foreign students, of humanities to simultaneously over-indulged and neglected teenagers in a fashionable preparatory school, and of English literature to extremely pregnant schoolgirls, back in the days when they sought refuge in Florence Crittenton Homes. (We all wept when David Copperfield was orphaned.) Finally there was an evening course in technical German for a roomful of electrical engineers (with a few chemists thrown in) – an exercise in mutual support, if ever there was one.

When I began the process of ordination to the priesthood I thought I was shedding the skin of my teacher identity and 'giving up' a life I had loved. As a priest, I envisioned myself working in a parish or possibly in a chaplaincy; ironically, I find myself back in the classroom and rejoice to be there. All the past experience has contributed to my present work and ministry; and I am surrounded by a cloud of witnesses – Peggy sitting patiently on the lowest porch step while I drill her on the three tables; the polite Japanese businessmen to whom I tried to demonstrate the difference between L and R; and all the classes of German students who couldn't quite catch my enthusiasm for adjective endings or the difference between dative and accusative. I realise I am, at least in part, a priest because I am a teacher; that my years as a teacher were years of preparation and that nothing has been wasted or lost.

I know that teaching itself is a holy calling, and so it is that teachers and spiritual directors are linked in my mind and in my practice. I am still a teacher and will remain so until the end. Please God, I have learned something about the difference between authority and power since those days of the porch-step school. Please God, I will go on tasting the joys of shared enterprise and discovery.

I still spend considerable time in classrooms, and syllabuses and reading lists still claim some of my attention. These days I am usually able to avoid limiting and defining intellectual and spiritual effort by assigning letter grades, but within the seminary framework I must nevertheless pronounce judgment: credit or no credit, pass or fail. Increasingly, however, I am aware that I am most fully a teacher when I meet with someone for spiritual direction. Increasingly, too, I am aware that what I teach cannot be neatly stated in catalogue course descriptions and that my work is infinitely more complex and subtle than the mere imparting of information.

Occasionally, people will seek spiritual direction when they might more suitably attend an inquirers' class or read a theological textbook. I can tell them without apology that intellectual curiosity about the faith is better satisfied elsewhere than in the spiritual direction relationship. Nor do I teach methods of prayer, even though I stand ready to help directees find the ways and rhythms that are most fruitful for them.

So what does the spiritual director teach?

In the simplest and also most profound terms, the spiritual director is simultaneously a learner and a teacher of discernment. What is happening? Where is God in this person's life? What is the story? Where does this person's story fit in our common Christian story? How is the Holy Spirit at work in this person's life? What's missing?

The first step in discernment is perception. The director is deeply attentive to the person sitting across the holy space, open and permeable to all that is said and unsaid, revealed and hidden. More important, by example and by judicious interpretation, she helps the directee towards equal openness and attentiveness. Together they look, listen and wait. The work of perception is not easy or automatic: we usually see what we want to see or expect to see. Especially when we seek to discern the action of the Holy Spirit in our lives, we expect the dramatic, even the spectacular. In this we resemble Naaman the leper. A powerful general, he travelled from Syria to seek healing from the prophet Elisha, who did not meet him in person but sent a messenger to tell him to wash himself in the river Jordan. Outraged at the almost offhand simplicity of the proposed treatment, he exclaimed:

Behold, I thought he [the prophet himself] would surely come out to me, and stand, and call on the name of the Lord his God, and wave his hand over the place. . . Are not Abana and Pharpar, the rivers of Damascus, better than all the rivers of Israel? Could I not wash in them, and be clean?[2]

The directee, similarly, may be quick to reject the homely, the ordinary, and the near-at-hand. Here the director as teacher can serve as a guide, gently pointing out the signs that are simultaneously hidden and obvious.

The second step in the work of discernment is judgment: what one does with the perception. What are the next steps for dealing with the insight that has come? It is important to focus on the **next** steps, despite the temptation to operate on a grander scale. It is human to want to wait for optimum conditions: I'll begin to pray again in Lent or after I have written this exam or maybe when I have fully recovered from this cold. I'll put my spiritual house in order as soon as things get straightened out at the office. I'll think about God again as soon as the baby sleeps through the night or goes to kindergarten or gets his driver's licence. One of the major teachings the director can offer – and offer again and again – is the value of the present moment. The fruits of discernment may be enjoyed far into the future, but the material of perception and the attendant judgment are to be found in the here and now, in the everydayness of the directee's life.

The director's task is twofold: he must himself be capable of discernment, able to put himself out of the way and be fully present to the person sitting opposite. At the same time, by encouragement and example, he helps the directee to develop and trust her own powers of discernment. This means that she must be able to look at herself, abandon her defences, and face up to hard questions. It may be more comfortable and considerably easier **not** to know what the Holy Spirit is up to.

The great model: Jesus the teacher

The great model for all teachers, and certainly for teachers who are spiritual directors, is Jesus himself. In the four gospels there are over forty references to him as teacher, and just skimming through them is an enlightening exercise. We learn that he

[2] 2 Kings 5:11–12.

taught 'as one who had authority' (Matthew 7:29; Mark 1:22).
We know that sometimes his teachings were painful, scarcely
to be received by his hearers as 'good news' – 'And he began to
teach them that the Son of man must suffer many things, and
be rejected . . . and be killed, and after three days rise again'
(Mark 8:31). And we note the rhythm of his teaching: he taught
in the 'corrrect' and predictable places, such as the temple and
the synagogue, but he also taught at the dinner table and as
he walked along the road. His methods were varied – stories,
parables, hard questions, koan-like sayings, and authoritative
pronouncements. He used visual aids: when the Pharisees
sought to entrap him in a discussion about the lawfulness of
paying taxes to Caesar, he asked them to show him a coin: 'And
they brought him a coin. And Jesus said to them, "Whose like-
ness and inscription is this?" They said, "Caesar's." Then he
said to them, "Render therefore to Caesar the things that are
Caesar's, and to God the things that are God's." '[3] The simplicity and concreteness of his response cut through all
entanglements. When his questioners heard it, they 'marvelled'
and departed.

He taught also by indirection and silence, notably in the story
of the woman taken in adultery, when his studied inattention
must have infuriated those who wished to catch him out in theological or legal error:

> The scribes and the Pharisees brought a woman who had
> been caught in adultery, and placing her in the midst they
> said to him, 'Teacher, this woman has been caught in the
> act of adultery. Now in the law Moses commanded us to
> stone such. What do you say about her?' . . . Jesus bent
> down and wrote with his finger on the ground. And as they
> continued to ask him, he stood up and said to them, 'Let
> him who is without sin among you be the first to throw a
> stone at her.' And once more he bent down and wrote with
> his finger on the ground. But when they heard it, they went
> away, one by one, beginning with the eldest.[4]

Current jargon would say that he refused to get hooked. Certainly by his silence he forced his questioners to stop playing
games, to abandon both legal quibbles and the urge to violence,
and to look within themselves.

[3] Matthew 22:19–21.
[4] John 8:3–9.

From the gospels we learn that teaching is a dangerous activity: while Pilate finds no crime in Jesus, his accusers 'were urgent, saying, "He stirs up the people, teaching throughout all Judea, from Galilee even to this place" ' (Luke 23:4–5). Jesus' teaching is clearly subversive, perhaps as all transformative work is subversive, a good point to be borne in mind by all who undertake the risky business of spiritual direction.

When Jesus is called 'teacher' by those especially close to him there is a special flavour of mingled intimacy and deference in the address. So in Luke's account of his anointing by 'a woman of the city, who was a sinner' he recognises the unspoken criticism in the mind of his host and says, 'Simon, I have something to say to you.' And the Pharisee answered, 'What is it, Teacher?' Jesus responds by citing a hypothetical case drawn from the world of commerce and hence far removed from the emotionally laden and sensuous scene before them. He invites Simon, a practical man, to solve a problem:

> 'A certain creditor had two debtors; one owed five hundred denarii, and the other fifty. When they could not pay, he forgave them both. Now which of them will love him more?' Simon answered, 'The one, I suppose, to whom he forgave more.' And he said to him, 'You have judged rightly.'[5]

At first glance it appears that Jesus is teaching his host about the woman – her right to be present, to approach Jesus, to receive forgiveness. Then he shifts the focus to Simon,

> 'Do you see this woman? I entered your house, you gave me no water for my feet, but she has wet my feet with her tears and wiped them with her hair. You gave me no kiss, but from the time I came in she has not ceased to kiss my feet. You did not anoint my head with oil, but she has anointed my feet with ointment. Therefore I tell you, her sins, which are many, are forgiven, for she loved much; but he who is forgiven little, loves little.'[6]

When Jesus asks 'Do you see this woman?' he is really commanding, 'Look at yourself.' This is indeed a story of spiritual direction, with the relationship clearly defined. Simon, the

---

[5] Luke 7:37, 40–43.
[6] Luke 7:44–47.

powerful and wealthy host, expects to hear truth from his teacher, and Jesus' reproach blends toughness with affection.

As spiritual directors we still encounter Simon's descendants. They are people of good taste who play by the rules. In their way, like Simon, they are generous and open to God. (The Pharisee, after all, invited Jesus to eat with him.) But also like Simon, they cannot believe that God could be guilty of bad taste or poor judgment. With Simon, they think, 'If this man were a prophet, he would have known who and what sort of woman this is who is touching him, for she is a sinner.' As a good teacher Jesus leads him to discernment, to a clear understanding of his own perceptions and the skewed harshness of his judgments.

My friend Trevor would have been at home at the Pharisee's table. He is a man of impeccable taste, for whom life is an aesthetic experience. Whether dinner party or liturgy, things must be done correctly and graciously. Trevor is not really a directee but seeks me out occasionally for a spiritual chat. Recently he called me, filled with 'righteous' anger at his rector, an earthy man who is more at home at a kitchen table than in a salon. The rector's chief sin seemed to be occasional use of salty language, providing earthenware crockery rather than china at the parish coffee hour, and a willingness to embrace the 'marginal elements' in the parish. It was as if Trevor were saying, 'If God were really God and if you were any sort of discerning priest, both of you would know who and what sort of man this is who is touching you, for he shouldn't be in the club!' I didn't do as well as Jesus in getting Trevor to see himself. He was still choked with rage when our conversation ended. Unlike Simon, he is not ready to hear what God – either in his own heart or speaking through the imperfect medium of a spiritual friend/ director – has to say to him. So he cannot ask, 'What is it, Teacher?'

There is another glimpse of Jesus as teacher in his relationship with Mary of Bethany. In Luke's account (10:38–41) she sits at his feet and listens to his teaching. This is not a position of subservience, but rather the posture of the pupil or disciple. There is much that is left unsaid in the brief passage, yet the depth of spiritual intimacy is clear. I find myself wanting to know more, to flesh out the story, and to learn the particulars of Jesus' teaching and her learning at his feet. The scene has been the subject of too many bad sermons contrasting the behaviour of Mary with that of her practical, housewifely sister.

If nothing else, it is an invitation, particularly to women, to claim the posture of receptivity and learning and to open themselves to the work of discernment.

An even richer paradigm of spiritual direction as teaching is found in the encounter of Jesus with the Samaritan woman.[7] In many ways she is the opposite of Simon the Pharisee: as a woman and a Samaritan she is relegated to society's margins, a throwaway person. Yet Jesus initiates a conversation with her. By asking for a drink of water he acknowledges his own need and invites her to minister to him. So the conversation begins in practical, down-to-earth terms and then moves rapidly from physical to spiritual concerns, with water, symbol of refreshment and cleansing, as its unifying symbol.

Once again the object of the teaching is self-knowledge: Jesus is helping the woman to look deeply into herself and to discover her thirst for God. He does not challenge her to deal intellectually or solve a hypothetical question, as he did with the Pharisee, but he offers her a great gift:

> Jesus said to her, 'Every one who drinks of this water [from the well] will thirst again, but whoever drinks of the water that I shall give him will never thirst; the water that I shall give him will become in him a spring of water welling up to eternal life.' The woman said to him, 'Sir, give me this water, that I may not thirst, nor come here to draw.'[8]

Without her telling him, Jesus knows this woman. He surprises her with his knowledge of her sexual life, an area that is very personal, private and potentially shameful. Yet she experiences his candour as liberating, for she leaves her water jar and goes to tell the whole city of her meeting with this prophet who has identified himself to her as the Messiah. John tells us, 'Many Samaritans from that city believed in him because of the woman's testimony, "He told me all that I ever did" ' (v. 39). She does not feel found out or accused, but rather – for the first time – truly known as herself. Now she is free to know herself, see herself, and be herself. In this new freedom she too becomes a teacher and brings good news to her neighbours, leading them on the first step towards self-knowledge.

Spiritual direction is often slow work. Again and again I counsel patience, both to myself and to my students: 'Wait.

[7] John 4:4–42.
[8] John 4:13–15.

Don't push. Take your time. It will unfold gradually.' But the conversation of Jesus with the Samaritan woman is filled with an almost breathless directness. Jesus gets right to the point: 'What I can give you will become in you a spring of water welling up to eternal life.' And she is equally direct: 'Sir, give me this water.' She is ready to articulate her own needs and to hear the truth about herself. And consequently she is able to hear the truth about Jesus: 'The woman said to him, "I know that Messiah is coming (he who is called Christ); when he comes, he will show us all things." Jesus said to her, "I who speak to you am he." '[9]

There is an important message for spiritual directors in this story: we may find our most receptive directees among the outcasts, those who live at the economic, social or ecclesial edges. These are people who have little to lose and everything to gain. Perhaps they are outcast by birth, chance or choice. But when Jesus asks the Samaritan woman to give him a drink he is telling us that there are no outcasts, that the category is artificial and dehumanising.

Like Simon the Pharisee, the Samaritan woman lives on among us. Sometimes she is well dressed and seems to belong, then reveals her marginality when she lets us glimpse her carefully concealed despair, depression or addiction. Sometimes we have pushed her to the edges because of ethnicity, sexual orientation or poverty. If we work at it, we can walk through our days and never see her.

Not long ago I met the Samaritan woman on an underground train. It had been a long day, filled with intense conversations and other people's pain. I didn't want to talk to anybody, and I certainly didn't want to listen to anybody. I expected to practise the cure of souls from eight to five, but now I was off duty. I looked forward to the anonymity of the journey, to immersing myself in my paperback.

Then a shabby, dishevelled, not very clean woman sat down beside me. I thought, how can I escape? She's already eyeing my clerical collar; she's spotted me for a soft touch. Sure enough, she started to talk: How are you, sister? And then the words rushed out. In a matter of minutes I seemed to have heard the story of her life, her struggle with addiction, her hopes for a new beginning in a rehabilitation centre. I knew I wasn't off duty after all, so I said the right things and felt **very** holy to

[9] John 4:25–26.

be so kind to this disposable person. When she got ready to leave, I knew she was going to ask for money and assure me that it was going for nourishing food, not drugs or alcohol. I went through my inner argument: should I, shouldn't I come up with a quarter, maybe two quarters? Then, as she stood up, she leaned close to me and pressed a subway token in my hand. 'God bless you, sister.' And she was gone.

I had failed to recognise her. My day and my energies had been spent with 'the right people', those who take showers and keep appointments. It had been a good day – at least, I had probably done no harm. But in retrospect I know that the woman on the underground was thirsty, not for more drugs or alcohol but for a sip of the water that would become in her a spring welling up to eternal life. I had responded with amiable platitudes; but in spite of me she was able to discern Christ in our midst. There was life in her gift to me, and I felt that she 'knew everything I ever did' and that it was all right.

Desert teachers

In their extreme asceticism and apparent denial of the goodness of creation, the fathers and mothers of the fourth-century desert seem unlikely mentors for spiritual directors in the late-twenti-eth-century West. Bizarre and often cantankerous, they would be out of place in the well-groomed respectability of our churches. (Abba Pambo said, 'The monk should wear a gar-ment of such a kind that he could throw it out of his cell and no one would steal it from him for three days.')[10] Yet as spiritual directors they were educators in the truest sense of the word, in that they drew forth from their followers insights and under-standing inherently present. True learning came from looking inward as one faced oneself (and God) in solitude: 'Go, sit in your cell, and your cell will teach you everything.'[11]

They taught by the example of their own lives as well as by their cryptic, koan-like counsel. Abba Isaac tells of his search as a young man for a spiritual master. Twice he attached him-self to more experienced abbas, ready to live in their households and to serve them. But they did not tell him what to do; rather, **they** served **him**. Isaac turned to other abbas for counsel:

They came and said to him [the second abba approached

[10] Ward, p. 197.
[11] Ibid. p. 139.

by Isaac], 'Abba, the brother has come to your holiness in order to help you. Why do you never tell him anything?' The old man said to them, 'Am I a cenobite, that I should give him orders? As far as I am concerned, I do not tell him anything, but if he wishes he can do what he sees me doing.' From that moment on I [Isaac] took the initiative and did what the old man was about to do. As for him, what he did, he did in silence; so he taught me to work in silence.[12]

They were willing to be silent, indeed were comfortable in the creative tension of silence. Like Theodore of Pherme, they could resist being made into gurus and were quite happy to be themselves:

'I meet people as they find me.' Then he said to his disciple, 'If someone comes to see me, do not say anything out of human respect, but if I am eating, say to him, "He is eating"; and if I am sleeping, say to him, "He is sleeping".'[13]

Most of the spiritual directors of the desert were men, but one of the few women, Amma Theodora, writes about teachers in words directly applicable to twentieth-century spiritual directors:

. . . a teacher ought to be a stranger to the desire for domination, vain-glory, and pride; one should not be able to fool him by flattery, nor blind him by gifts, nor conquer him by the stomach, nor dominate him by anger; but he should be patient, gentle, and humble as far as possible; he must be tested and without partisanship, full of concern, and a lover of souls.[14]

There is nothing bizarre or cantankerous about Theodora! She knew nothing of the vocabulary of projection, transference or counter-transference, but she knew how the director-teacher could get caught in self-deception and lose her loving detachment in a relationship of spiritual intimacy. As directors, our warning signals should sound when directees bring us adulation rather than basic human respect and when they try to elevate us to sanctity. Rarely do directees attempt to blind me

[12] Ibid. pp. 99–100.
[13] Ibid. p. 78.
[14] Ibid. pp. 83–4.

by gifts, or conquer me by the stomach – but I resist invitations that are purely social and that can trivialise the relationship. Over the years, as directees turn into friends, I find that we can continue to work together as long as we keep our lunch dates quite distinct from direction sessions.

When Theodora warns against being dominated by anger, no doubt she was thinking of her own anger, since the abbas and the ammas of the desert struggled constantly against this emotion. (Abba Agathon said, 'A man who is angry, even if he were to raise the dead, is not acceptable to God.')[15] As a spiritual director, however, I am in greater danger from other people's anger and my reaction to it. Most of us want to be liked and are consequently reluctant to offend. Since most people have trouble expressing anger, especially in anything to do with God, we are often faced with testing behaviour or denial in our directees when they come to us full of – often misplaced – rage. How long do we let it go on? How do we repond, combining love and truth? How can we use the directee's anger? Sometimes the air is cleared when I remark mildly, 'You seem pretty angry today.'

With Michelle, desperately lonely and still unhealed from a childhood with an abusive mother, the situation is more complicated. I know she sees me as a 'good' mother, but that she fears I might turn on her. We have worked together long enough for her to want to test the relationship, so about a year ago she pushed me more and more towards confrontation. She was being consumed by rage and jealousy, which she dared not name and attempted to mask by a pious sweetness. She resisted relationships and experiences that would force her, like Simon the Pharisee, to stop looking at others in harsh judgment and to see herself. The others – her classmates, fellow-parishioners, members of her prayer group – she implied were nice people but not on her level. If I did not name her spiritual grandiosity (masking an abysmal absence of self-worth), I was guilty of complicity. So I spoke some hard truths, then said: 'You're probably really angry with me, and that's all right. It won't hurt me, and I won't get angry with you.' With rage in her eyes but in a soft, sweet voice, she assured me that she could never be angry with me. And then she disappeared for six months.

According to Amma Theodora, the director should be without partisanship. We all want to be favourite children: God's

[15] Ibid. p. 23.

favourites, our parents' favourites, our director's favourite –
even when the relationship is one of mutuality and not quasi-
parental. (I recall with shame my own sense of betrayal years
ago when I learned by chance that I shared my director with a
woman I considered well-intentioned but not very bright.
'What can she see in **her**?' was – *mea culpa* – my initial reaction.)
In the small world of spiritual direction we often know our
directees in other contexts, and our directees are likely to know,
possibly dislike, and even feel contempt for each other. Strict
observance of confidentiality can help us towards impartiality.
If we cannot be open to the directee and even find ourselves
taking sides, it is past time to refer him to someone else, taking
of course full responsibility for the deterioration of the relationship.

Perhaps most important of all, Theodora urges that the
teacher-director be a lover of souls. Although this is not
common American-English parlance, it has gained currency
through the inclusion of an Orthodox-inspired collect in the
1979 Book of Common Prayer,[16] which makes clear that God is
the true lover of souls. For the teacher-director the love of souls
is a detached, contemplative love that wants nothing in return.

The question

There are many questions in spiritual direction – asked,
implied, answered, and unanswered – but as the story gets told
and the extraneous stripped away, it is clear that **one** question
lies at its heart: 'Good Teacher, what must I do to inherit eternal life?'

It is rarely phrased so baldly, and the person seeking spiritual
direction may not be aware that this IS the question. The director knows, of course, that the yearning for God and relationship
with God – eternal life – underlie everything in the work of
direction and knit the disparate parts together. For the directee
the question may emerge in sharp focus as trust develops, and
the work continues. But the question was there all along.

Mark's gospel account of the rich young man is a paradigm
for spiritual direction, especially for spiritual direction as teaching. The words of address acknowledge the hierarchical

---

[16] O Lord our God, accept the fervent prayers of your people; in the multitude
of your mercies, look with compassion upon us and all who turn to you for
help; for you are gracious, O lover of souls, and to you we give glory, Father,
Son, and Holy Spirit (The Book of Common Prayer, NY, The Church Hymnal
Corporation 1979, p. 395).

relationship: the petitioner looks to the teacher – the **good** teacher – for an answer which he cannot find within himself. There is also affectionate connection; it is implicit that the good teacher will have the interest of the questioner at heart. It seems simplistic to note that one can be a teacher only in relationship, that the whole purpose of teaching is to enable another to make his own discoveries. So the hierarchy is a gentle and perhaps transitory one, and the teacher's apparent power is just that – apparent. As in Mark's story, the questioner must be free to deal with and even learn to love the question.

Mark tells us that 'Jesus looking upon him loved him'. The teacher-pupil relationship is based on love – or should be. We tend to be miserly with our love and to assume its propriety only in close personal relationships. Most damaging of all, we confuse love with warm, mushy, entangling feelings. Such is not the detached, clear-eyed love of the teacher.

I find myself wondering whether the man knew that Jesus loved him. At that moment, probably not! One of the hard tasks of spiritual direction is to speak the truth in love:

> . . . speaking the truth in love, we are to grow up in every way into him who is the head, into Christ, from whom the whole body, joined and knit together by every joint with which it is supplied, when each part is working properly, makes bodily growth and upbuilds itself in love.[17]

We may spare the very fragile, those who have already more reality than they can bear and are not yet ready to hear the truth. It is sometimes hard to sit with an insight, yet we may say nothing, or we may measure out manageable bits of truth. But with the strong and spiritually mature we need not be so cautious.

I learned this in a conversation with Karen, who had come to talk about her growing sense of vocation to the ordained ministry. I knew enough about her family situation and her husband's implacable hostility to the Church to know that her marriage could not withstand the strain if she decided to pursue her vocation. What I didn't know was Karen's great inner toughness, almost ruthlessness. So I said mildly, rather like a spiritual agony aunt trying to make life run smoothly, 'A person really needs family support, especially a spouse's support, before she starts off on this road.' Karen's eyes flashed, 'I'm

---

[17] Ephesians 4:15–16.

talking about a call from **God**!' I knew then that this was a woman who didn't want minimum doses of sugar-coated truth, so I said, 'Excuse me for not saying directly what I meant. You know that your marriage probably won't survive if you pursue the call to ordination, don't you?' Karen signed and whispered, 'I know.' (She has moved to another town and we have lost touch. But the last time we spoke she was still struggling with the implications of her call.)

Had the unnamed seeker in Mark's gospel come to me I might have been tempted to comfort him: 'You're really doing all right. Most people wouldn't be able to keep all those commandments. So just keep on doing what you're doing, and don't worry about eternal life.' But Jesus knew that this man was ready to hear the truth, and so he gave **the** answer to **the** question. And the man's 'countenance fell, and he went away sorrowful; for he had great possessions'.

Here again Jesus is the teacher of discernment. He is saying, 'Look at your life. Look at your treasure. See yourself.' What were the great possessions? What are the great possessions which weigh down our directees, which intrude themselves between the seeker and God? Most obviously the man was wealthy in a material sense; and no doubt in first-century Palestine as in the twentieth-century world, money management could demand total commitment. Wealth is an attractive idol, easier to get hold of than God, and promising comfort and security. Unlike God, it can be measured and manipulated. But there are other possessions which cause the seeker to go away sorrowful. It is hard to let go of carefully constructed identities, especially clerical and 'spiritual' ones. (Perhaps this explains why so many clergy are unreliable as directees.) It is hard to let go of a lifetime of accumulated addictions, not only addictions to harmful chemicals but also to frantic busyness, mind- and spirit-numbing leisure activities and unhealthy relationships. And it is especially hard to let go of the freedom of spiritual irresponsibility, even when drifting aimlessly, trying to ignore the magnetic pull of of God's love, has its own special pain.

The story of the rich and sorrowful man makes clear that spiritual direction is not to be undertaken lightly. Those who see it as yet another avenue towards self-improvement and self-discovery may be surprised at the demands made upon them if they persevere and 'follow all the commandments'. They may expect a pat on the head; instead the demands increase as commitment increases. As the work deepens in its intensity it is important for the spiritual director-teacher to remember what is being taught: to look at oneself without flinching and then to act and be accordingly.

Sometimes the cost is too much, and the directee chooses to leave the relationship. Often the reasons for termination are not articulated, or those given are secondary. But a colleague told me the poignant story of a woman who told him she wasn't coming back. She was well-to-do, leisured, educated – a good woman who observed all the commandments. As my colleague met her regularly for spiritual direction he was delighted to watch her grow and find her true voice. She was being transformed before his eyes, and he sensed that she stood on a threshold. He didn't know what the next step would be; it might involve a radical change in her life-style. Or the change might be deeper: outwardly she would be the same, but her whole life would radiate from a deep inner commitment. And then she said, 'I won't be back. This is costing too much. I'm going to have to change and I don't want to change. I like my life the way it is.' I don't know about the woman, but my friend came away sorrowful.

Jesus was able to let the man go. This is a hard lesson for spiritual directors, maybe because we fear failure. In other words we have a prideful stake in being right, being successful, pointing out the next best step. It is hard to let people go, hard to entrust them to God's care – which might mean that our time together will bear fruit decades into the future, but that they will wander in a far country and eat husks until then.

Mark doesn't tell us any more about the rich and sorrowful seeker after eternal life. I harbour the secret hope that maybe he came back!

The hunger to be known

If the yearning for God prompts the primary question of spiritual direction, 'What must I do to inherit eternal life?' the concomitant yearning to be known is of almost equal urgency. This is not to be confused with egocentricity or self-centredness. Again and again I meet people who are unwilling, indeed unable to believe themselves capable of God's love and forgiveness. At times this attitude reflects a kind of Faustian pride: I am so bad or so worthless that I alone, of all creation, am closed off from God's love. But behind this defence is the painful inability to believe that they are **known** to God, that is, that they exist for God. It appears almost more difficult for them to believe in their own existence – their true existence in God – than to believe in the existence of God.

In this context I am greatly indebted to Parker Palmer. In *To Know as We are Known: The Spirituality of Education*, he is writing about education *per se*, but much of what he says is applicable to the spiritual direction relationship. Taking his basic text from 1 Corinthians 13:12 – 'Now we are seeing a dim reflection in a mirror; but then we shall be seeing face to face. The knowledge that I have now is imperfect; but then I shall know as fully as I am known' – Palmer is primarily concerned with overcoming the gap between subject and object, the knower and the known. He notes the etymological connection between 'truth' and 'troth' and states:

> To know something or someone in truth is to enter troth with the known, to rejoin with new knowing what our minds have put asunder. To know in truth is to become betrothed, to engage the known with one's whole self, an engagement one enters with attentiveness, care, and good will. To know in truth is to allow one's self to be known as well, to be vulnerable to the challenges and changes any true relationship brings. To know in truth is to enter into the life of that which we know and to allow it to enter into ours. Truthful knowing weds the knower and the known; even in separation, the two become part of each other's life and fate.[18]

To know in truth, then, is to allow one's self to be known. This is the truth that became incarnate in Jesus Christ, a truth that is known not in abstraction but in relationship. The shared commitment to truth ensures that the spiritual direction relationship is one of true mutuality, for both director and directee must allow themselves to be known. This marks one of the major differences between spiritual direction and psychotherapy: the director must be willing to be known – not just by her credentials, affiliations and titles, but known in her vulnerability and limitations as a child of God.

Similarly, a directee must be willing to be known, to lay aside his – possibly beautiful and useful – masks one by one. Despite all good intentions, this is not easy work. Those highly committed to the institutional Church – clergy, seminarians and all

---

[18] London, Harper & Row 1986, p. 31.

who have a position to uphold – may be reluctant to reveal their doubts and deficiencies, their spiritual feet of clay. Then, too, spiritual direction attracts a disproportionate number of introverts, who require a great deal of time and patience to reach the level of trust necessary for self-revelation. A friend once likened doing spiritual direction with them to coaxing a deer out of the forest: you watch it peering out between the trees, occasionally venturing into the meadow, but a sudden move on your part can send it dashing back into the woods. In a culture that regards extroversion as the norm and often equates ready self-disclosure with honesty, it is easy to dismiss the introvert as spiritually shallow or to grow impatient with what seems like teasing behaviour. The director needs to listen carefully for hints and then to follow them up. The very private introvert may assume that transitions and shifts are clear, even when they are not articulated. I have learned to ask questions, to press for clarification when provocative statements are made and then left hanging. 'Tell me more' or 'I don't quite understand' are usually sufficient to bring clarification. Sometimes, however, the deer runs back into the thicket and the director is left to wait patiently for the next foray into self-disclosure.

Only by letting ourselves be known, to each other and our deepest selves, can we feel the assurance that we are indeed known to God. If this inner work is done in spiritual direction, there will be an inevitable effect on the relation of the individual to the rest of Creation. When he allows himself to be known to himself, another, and to God, the directee will see that the world (including his fellow human creatures) is not an object to be manipulated and analysed. Instead he will be aware of the web of relationship, connecting him to all Creation.

The spiritual director as teacher does not make the connections, although she may make observations, give hints (but without being manipulative), and ask the right questions. Her supportive presence sets the directee free to make the connections; and inner and outer work turn out to be all of a piece.

With E. F. Schumacher, I lament our secular (and all too often our ecclesiastical) leaders' failure to do this needed inner work of knowing and being known, along with their unfortunate unawareness of what inner work is:

World crises multiply and everybody deplores the shortage, or even total lack, of 'wise' men and women, unselfish leaders, trustworthy counsellors, etc. It is hardly rational to expect such high qualities from people who have never done any *inner work* and would not even understand what is meant by the words.[19]

The ancient Celts had just such 'wise men and women' and 'trustworthy counsellors' in the person of the *anmchara*, the soul friend to whom kings and chieftains were voluntarily accountable. It is a breathtaking fantasy: what if there were spiritual directors/teachers in the Pentagon and White House and board rooms? What if the *anmchara* replaced or at least shared the influence of the legal adviser for the makers of decisions and those who wield power in the secular sphere?

Good teachers

While Jesus protests when the rich man addresses him as **good** teacher, we have all had sufficient experience of bad or mediocre teachers to know that, in our human finitude, we must strive to be as-good-as-possible teachers. The responsibility of doing spiritual direction is a heavy one, and the possibility for mischief is great.

A good teacher encourages play. Our culture has made leisure an industry but knows very little about play. Often what we call 'play' is compelled, competitive and compulsive. The aesthetic dimension of true play, its holy uselessness, goes against our cultural grain. Yet the German poet-philosopher Schiller says wisely, the human being is completely human only when he or she plays. And I am constantly struck by the proximity of 'play' and 'pray'; this is brought home to me in serendipitous messages from my word processor, when my fingers take on a life of their own and I find myself writing 'It will be necessary to play about this'.

This linking of play and prayer – and implicitly the linking of play with the work of contemplative living – is apparent in *The Cloud of Unknowing*. The author notes that it is not always possible to be at one's spiritual best: 'Sickness, afflictions of body and mind, and countless other necessities of nature will often leave you indisposed and keep you from its [contemplative prayer's] heights. *Yet, at the same time, I counsel you to remain*

[19] E. F. Schumacher, *A Guide for the Perplexed* (New York, Harper & Row 1977), p. 85.

at it always either in earnest or, as it were, playfully.'[20] These are reassuring words for directors/teachers as they try to help directees through periods of aridity, poor health, personal difficulties and distraction. Directees may make heavy going of it and add a load of self-blame to the burden they are already carrying. Others tend to slack off when it is not possible to maintain the level of spiritual intensity they have set for themselves, with the result that they turn away from spiritual direction at the time it would be of greatest support to them. The director can help them to remain at it 'as it were, playfully'. A light touch is called for: 'For the love of God, then, be careful and do not imprudently strain yourself at this work. Rely more on joyful enthusiasm than on sheer brute force. . . Do not impatiently snatch at grace like a greedy greyhound suffering from starvation.'[21]

The Cloud presents a delightful picture of prayer as play, a game of hide and seek with a playful parent God:

> I speak half playfully now, but try to temper the loud, crude sighing of your spirit and pretend to hide your heart's longing from the Lord. Perhaps you will scorn this as childish and frivolous but believe me, anyone who has the light to understand what I mean and the grace to follow it will experience, indeed, *the delight of the Lord's playfulness. For like a father frolicking with his son, he will hug and kiss one who comes to him with a child's heart.*[22]

The anonymous author of the *Ancrene Riwle* offers a similar picture of a playful God inviting a playful response:

> The sixth comfort is that our Lord, when he allows us to be tempted, is playing with us as a mother with her darling child. She runs away from him and hides, and leaves him on his own, and he looks around for her, calling 'Mama! Mama!' and crying a little, and then she runs out to him quickly, her arms outspread, and she puts them round him, and kisses him, and wipes his eyes. In the same way, our Lord sometimes leaves us alone for a while and withdraws his grace, his comfort and consolation, so that we find no pleasure in doing things well, and our heart's savour is gone. And yet, at that very moment our Lord is

[20] *The Cloud of Unknowing* and *The Book of Privy Counselling*, ed. William Johnston (NY, Image Books 1973), p. 100. My italics.
[21] Ibid. pp. 106–7.
[22] Ibid. p. 107. My italics.

not loving us any the less, but is doing this out of his great love for us.[23]

Play is simultaneously intense (just watch a four-year-old with Matchbox cars and a few bricks) and freeing. We are freed from our compulsion for right answers, freed from the need to acquire and achieve, freed from anxiety by the transitory nature of play. With imagination as the generous supplier of raw material, we can be rich beyond belief. Everything matters tremendously – and matters not at all.

Since it is hard to be heavily defended when engaged in true play, it is an excellent way of shedding our masks, of letting ourselves be known, of **unselfing**, in the classical language of spirituality. Play stretches us and helps to push out the boundaries; in spiritual direction it can provide gentle help in discarding icons that have turned into idols. For that matter, it can also provide the exhilarating energy with which – in our younger days – we knocked down brick structures and sand castles when they had served their purpose. Sometimes it can be just as much fun to smash our homemade idols!

So play has a real place in the serious work of spiritual direction, and I try to find ways to introduce it. This calls for gentle perseverance; for, even though some directees don't mind and even welcome 'penitential assignments', they are frightened at the prospect of play. So when I suggested that Alice made a list – minimum three items and maximum unlimited – to find ways in which God might delight in her, she declared that she couldn't think of one single thing. In fact even contemplating the exercise seemed presumptuous to her until I reminded her of the wonderful verse tucked in the middle of Psalm 18: 'He brought me out into an open place, he rescued me because he delighted in me'. I encouraged her to play with the idea, to pay attention to the small, seemingly trivial things that came into her mind. At our next meeting she announced with a smile that God might delight in her tennis game, that she had a pleasant voice, and that she had managed to complete college while working part-time. We were on our way! Grace proved more difficult. She lives – rather grimly – for her family and was angrily resistant when I suggested she played with a plan of what she would do if she had only herself to consider. 'Are you telling me to imagine that my family is dead?' she asked. Her resistance tells me a great deal about her image of God – and

[23] Tr. M. B. Salu (London, Burns & Oates, 1955), p. 134.

her true feelings about her family. I haven't been brave enough to suggest that verse of Psalm 18 to her yet.

Sometimes it helps the directee take the risk if I enter into the play, carefully, so that the directee does not feel compelled to imitate me but is free to find his own voice and images. This has proved effective in groups when the members get stuck in safe and pious platitudes. Once I was working with a group of women and suggested we played with the idea of God's names and images for us. We were having trouble getting past 'beloved child' and 'faithful servant' when I said, 'You know, I think God sees me as a little grey donkey, hardworking, pretty reliable, but awfully thick-headed.' After the laughter died down, we found that the group was flooded with images – powerful, comic, poignant. We were letting ourselves be known.

I have spoken of those who resist play in spiritual direction. Not surprisingly, these directees often combine a poor self-image with a tendency to 'spiritualise' everything. In other words they want to avoid the grittiness of everyday life and come to direction with the expectation of pious conversation divorced from all reality. With wicked humour the author of *The Cloud* says of such displays of piety: 'sometimes their eyes look like the eyes of wounded sheep near death' and goes on to counsel avoidance of the extreme and the eccentric, 'Far better a modest countenance, a calm, composed bearing, and a merry candour.'[24]

Here the spiritual director can help to sanctify the ordinary and restore naturalness – 'a merry candour'. This is better taught by example than precept, and the director can begin by demythologising himself. Perhaps, if he is ordained, he might substitute mufti for clerical dress for a meeting with the excessively spiritual. This is also a good time for some judicious self-revelation, connecting a life of prayer with the minutiae of the here and now. Sometimes it helps for the directee to know that I go to the grocery shop or visit my dentist. I still remember my daughter's surprise at meeting her nursery school teacher in the supermarket. It had not occurred to her that Miss Pat shopped, cooked and ate like an ordinary mortal. So an occasional bit of down-to-earth chat as we say goodbye can go a long way towards helping the directee remember that I, like Miss Pat, am an ordinary mortal.

[24] *The Cloud of Unknowing*, ed. Johnston, p. 116.

If there is a place for play in spiritual direction, there is obviously a place for laughter as well. Here caution is in order, for humour can be wounding; and wit can be used to avoid engagement with deep issues. But bearing these two dangers in mind, directors should not be afraid of laughter. It can be wonderfully cleansing and refreshing.

The whole purpose of play is to help the directee be most fully herself, to help her to know and be known, and move closer to the self-knowledge that underlies true humility.

A good teacher knows his/her pupils' limits. This calls for great sensitivity to timing, knowing when to speak and when to keep silent. It is tempting to say all that we know, to turn teaching into instruction. But we are not there to tell people things or to help them analyse and pin labels on themselves; rather, we are there to educate, literally to help them bring forth what is already there. The work of discernment is different with each directee: the newly baptised person, still in the euphoria of a conversion experience, merits different treatment from the senior seminarian who possesses a sophisticated theological vocabulary and a certain cynicism about the institutional Church. The former needs the gentle support of someone willing to share in his joy and to encourage him not to push on too quickly, lest he snap at grace like a greedy greyhound. The seminarian, on the other hand, may need to be challenged not to hide behind intellectual abstractions. She might welcome a certain toughness of approach that would be inappropriate with the newcomer.

It is part of my work at the Center for Christian Spirituality to interview people who are seeking a director and then to make a referral, sometimes to participants in our programmes and sometimes to other directors in the community. I usually spend about an hour getting to know them a bit and encouraging them to articulate their wishes and hopes. Again and again I hear, 'I need somebody who won't let me get away with anything, somebody tough. I don't want somebody who's just going to be nice to me.' When I first began this work I trembled inwardly and thought, 'This is a strong person who can see right through me and know that I'm a spiritual pussy-cat if not an outright wimp. Now who do I know who's **really** tough?' But now that I have heard variations of the same request dozens, even hundreds of times, I am better able to see the wounded, tentative seeker behind the bravado and to know that this is a person who feels unworthy of God's love. Not long ago I met Jean, an attractive, youngish woman who seemed to have it all: professional success, a reasonably secure marriage, handsome children. Her manner was friendly but brisk, her language precise. She hoped I would be able to refer her to a director who would challenge and confront her, not let her get away with anything. (Those words again!) I decided to take the risk, so after a moment I asked, 'Why are you afraid of gentleness, Jean?' Tears came into her eyes, and she shook her head.

This does not mean that the director should not combine candour with compassion and expect commitment and hard work from the directee. A good teacher demands accountability, which is why we usually learn better with a teacher than we do on our own, no matter what the subject matter. But this is a long and mutual accountability, with no place in it for fear or coercion. I am accountable to the directee, to whom I owe my attention, discretion and prayers. The directee is accountable in that she takes the relationship seriously, honours the director's gift of time and attention, and brings her best and truest self to the work.

A good teacher is always hopeful. I am convinced that much of the grimness of contemporary secular education exists because it is a loveless enterprise, from which no fruit is really expected. The teacher/director, on the other hand, is filled with hope for the directee. Seeing the potential for growth and transformation in even the least likely, he is willing to wait for fruition. In dark times his quiet hope can sustain the directee. This is the hopefulness of Dame Julian, who, without shrinking from pain and evil, knew that ultimately all would be well.

> He did not say: You will not be troubled, you will not be belaboured, you will not be disquieted; but he said: You will not be overcome. God wants us to pay attention to these words, and always to be strong in faithful trust, in well-being and in woe, for he loves and delights in us, and so he wishes us to love him and delight in him and trust greatly in him, and all will be well.[25]

In one of his homilies Gregory the Great depicts Jesus as a teacher who encourages and sustains hope. He speaks movingly of John's gospel account of Mary Magdalene's perseverance at the empty tomb:

> Why did she stoop down again, why did she want to look

[25] Julian of Norwich, *Showings*, p. 315.

again? It is never enough for a lover to have looked once, because love's intensity does not allow a lover to give up the search. Mary sought a first time and found nothing; she persevered in seeking, and so it happened that she found Jesus.[26]

How often do directees look into the empty tomb, even when they 'know' it is empty. This calls for patience on the part of the director and awareness that the directee is in the right place for now, even though it is painful to linger in a place that seems dead and fruitless – an empty tomb. Our tendency is to want to get on with it, whatever 'it' might be. We both see that the tomb is empty, so come on, let's go! But here the pupil is wise, knowing what she must do. She lingers, stoops to look in once again, and 'so it happened that she found Jesus'. This reminds me of my friend Ellen – I dare not call her a directee, for she is my teacher as much as I am hers. In her nineties and knowing that death is near, like Mary she perseveres in looking into the empty tomb. She does not fear death, but she yearns for a sense of the presence of God after a lifetime of seeking. For a time, with the false wisdom of relative youth and with great confidence in my supposed gift of discernment, I thought she was stuck and needed rescuing from her fruitless search. How could she doubt God's love for her? What more could she want? But I have learned to honour her faithfulness in looking into the empty tomb and to honour my position standing beside (and a little behind) her. She is looking for God, not finding God, but willing to go on waiting and looking.

Gregory reminds us of the centrality of Jesus' identity as teacher: 'Because Mary was called by name, she acknowledged her Creator, and called him at once *Rabboni, which means teacher.* He was at once the one she was outwardly seeking, and the one who was inwardly teaching her to seek him.'[27] In his appearance to Mary at the empty tomb Jesus reminds us powerfully of the object of his teaching and indeed of the teaching of all spiritual directors: he was 'inwardly teaching Mary to seek him'. Similarly our true work is not to impart information nor to support a change in the directee's life-style, however desirable these aims might be. Our work is to follow Christ's example and inwardly teach those who come to us to seek him. The prayer of Mary at the empty tomb and indeed of all engaged in the minis-

[26] Gregory the Great, Homily 22.
[27] Ibid.

try of spiritual direction might well be Julian's: 'God, of your goodness, give me yourself, for you are enough for me, and I can ask nothing which is less which can pay you full worship. And if I ask anything which is less, always I am in want, but only in you do I have everything.'[28]

A good teacher (like a good parent) is educating for maturity. Parents have done their work well when they are no longer needed. In spiritual direction the initially hierarchical relationship may turn into a rich spiritual friendship. This is not a sign that something has gone wrong, but it is important to acknowledge and celebrate the changed relationship. The friendship can continue, but the directee will eventually need to find a new director. The give-and-take between friends cannot substitute for the careful attentiveness of a lovingly distanced director.

A good teacher asks questions, but they must be the right questions. They should be questions that open doors and invite the directee to stretch and grow. Obviously one never asks questions out of curiosity nor to fill a silence that threatens to become uncomfortable. At times, however, clarification is needed; then a gentle question can be helpful to director and directee alike: 'Could you say a little more about that? Can you give me an example of what you mean by. . . ?' I am learning to notice statements that cry out for a clarifying question, especially when the directee is dealing with painful material or on the threshold of a new stage of awareness. Hints are dropped, bits of information are offered, and there is a disjointed quality in the narrative. It is almost as if the directee were saying: 'I left a piece out there. What I am saying doesn't make sense. Why don't you ask me about it?' The clarifying question is by no means probing or pouncing; a simple 'Help me understand what you are saying. Do you mean. . . ?' is almost always sufficient.

I am wary of falling into a false Socratic mode of questioning, an exercise in manipulation in which I know the conclusion before I begin and (subtly, I hope) manoeuvre the directee into saying what I expect to hear. This method might work well in academic settings, where logic is appropriately employed; but it has a chilling effect when the mysteries of the human soul are being explored. It presupposes a right answer, and in the

[28] Julian of Norwich, *Showings*, p. 184.

ministry of spiritual direction there are no right answers, only clearer vision and ever deeper questions.

In awareness of the mystery at the heart of spiritual direction, **the good teacher also encourages the directee to discover and embrace his own questions**. The Czech poet Rilke's *Letters to a Young Poet*, while ostensibly about the creative process, is equally valuable as a spiritual classic. It is a deceptively simple book about discernment and self-knowledge. Especially, in the fourth letter, he urges his reader

> to be patient towards all that is unsolved in your heart and to try to love the *questions themselves* like locked rooms and like books that are written in a very foreign tongue. Do not seek the answers, which cannot be given you because you would not be able to live them. And the point is, to live everything. *Live* the questions now.[29]

To love the questions is to engage them ever more deeply, to let go, and to risk. It is to struggle with the translation of 'books written in a very foreign tongue' – and to love the struggle. To live the question is to be willing to persevere at peering into the empty tomb. Directees who come to us wanting a quick fix of spiritual certainty will surely be disappointed.

A good teacher is willing and able to evaluate progress. Even as there are no right answers in spiritual direction, there are no report cards with letter grades. Yet our directees come to us – at least in part – for orientation, to try to understand where they are spiritually, how they got there, and perhaps what the next step might be.

When to give feedback in spiritual direction? In theory, I think regular times of mutual assessment are helpful, perhaps quarterly once the relationship is well established. In practice, however, I work pragmatically and often intuitively. Sometimes the directee will ask, 'What do you see? Tell me what you think.' There is a graced quality to the timing of these requests; almost always we have worked together long enough and intensively enough for me to be able to respond constructively.

Sometimes I offer feedback when the directee seems stuck, not persevering at looking into the empty tomb, but just plain stuck. She may have reached a plateau, where faithfulness doesn't seem to be enough. Discouraged, she feels as if she is

---

[29] Rainer Maria Rilke, *Letters to a Young Poet*, tr. M. D. Herter Norton (NY, Norton 1954), p. 35.

slipping backwards. Then it helps for the director to comment, as specifically as possible, on the growth and change that he has observed. This assessment should be an honest and realistic one, for the aim is not to make the directee feel good but to provide a helpful evaluation.

Occasionally the evaluation is a painful one. After working for some months with Helena I observed a pattern of envy in her relationship with women clergy. Helena aspired to ordination herself, but had been rejected by her diocese for the process. When we first met she was enthusiastic about the female curate in her parish, but then her adulation turned to harsh criticism. Helena moved to another parish, where the process repeated itself. When she told me she was thinking of changing parishes again and commented (as if introducing a new topic) that the young woman assistant was a poor preacher and **very** hard to talk to, I knew it was time to point out what I was seeing. Helena hasn't changed parishes again; she is somewhat more realistic about the capabilities and deficiencies of the women clergy, and considerably more aware of the depths of her own disappointment and its potential for poisoning her relationship with others.

Feedback is especially welcome to those who have had a profound religious experience and are reluctant to name it. I never cease to be surprised at our circumspection in speaking of God, particularly a sense of God's immanence, even in spiritual direction. Jeff had come to me seeking a referral to a director. He was down-to-earth, matter-of-fact and definitely not unbalanced. But as he talked it was clear to me that he was gifted with mystical experiences and was afraid to talk about them, probably for fear that he would be seen as eccentric, if not downright demented. Finally I said, 'It sounds as if you are very blessed. Lots of people would envy your experience of God's nearness.' He looked surprised, then laughed with relief when I said, 'I guess it's safe to say the dreaded M-word – mystical.' He still holds his secret very close, an indication to me that his mystical tendencies are healthy and genuine. The M-word has become a code expression between us.

A good teacher is vulnerable. She bears her own partially healed wounds and scars and counts them among her gifts. Annie Sullivan, Helen Keller's teacher, provides a good model. When she began to work with Helen, Annie herself was young and seriously impaired. But her own handicap made her available to the tragically isolated child and enabled her to make demands which the 'whole' and 'healthy' members of the Keller family were unable to make. Helen's name for this woman, who enabled her to know and be known, was 'Teacher'.

A lot of us are Annie Sullivans when we begin the work of spiritual direction, spiritually if not chronologically young and afflicted with imperfect vision. It is tempting to deny our gifts for this ministry and to wait, in the expectation that some day we will be ready – strong, unblemished and wise. How do you know when you are ready to be a spiritual director? The best indication is that people begin to seek you out to talk about their deepest concerns, that they are willing to lay aside their masks when they are with you. This can be a heady experience, and one should be wary if it is **too** enjoyable. It cannot be said too often that the director needs to be humble, that is, to know his own small place in the great order of things. Given true humility and the safeguard of having his own director, the reluctant novice can grow and deepen his skills in the ministry.

In her own vulnerability, **a good teacher is always a learner, not a finished product**. She is willing to share herself, to acknowledge that she has travelled and is still travelling the same road as the directee. While the role of guru may be tempting, it is a great burden to live among others who think that you have arrived. I still recall the sense of freedom that came over me when, as a quite young college instructor, I was able to stand before a class and say, 'I honestly don't know because I have never thought about this question. But we can check it out together.' That was the day I stopped being an instructor and began to be a teacher.

In the seminar room and in spiritual direction, danger arises when the teacher stops learning. The mutuality of the teacher-learner relationship is lost, as one has and gives, the other is empty and receives. Instead, as Aelred points out, there should be a circularity in the exchange: 'Speak freely, therefore, and entrust to your friend all your cares and thoughts, that you may both learn and teach, give and receive, pour out and drink in.'[30] It is one of the clichés of the teaching profession to exclaim (with patently false humility), 'The students taught me more than I ever taught them.' But the direction relationship is truly a two-way street, even when roles are clearly defined.

So the good teacher avoids becoming an ossified 'authority' by remaining a learner. The teacher who lets herself be taught

[30] Aelred, p. 52.

will always be aware of what the other is experiencing and know what it is like to be in the learner's position. (It was an illuminating and salutary experience for me when, after years in the classroom, I resumed piano lessons. But this was a pale foreshadowing of what it was like, at the age of fifty, to move from the teacher's position of authority behind the desk and join my fellow juniors in seminary.) Like Annie Sullivan, the teacher who is being taught combines a challenging toughness with great love.

The teacher of prayer

The purpose of spiritual direction resembles Merton's statement regarding the purpose of education, quoted at the beginning of this chapter – with one major alteration. The purpose of spiritual direction is to show (or help the person discover) how to define himself authentically and spontaneously in relation to his world, but more importantly to **God**. That is a huge and seemingly amorphous undertaking, the work of a lifetime. But within this framework the director is called upon to help in specific ways, to teach in an almost traditional manner.

Almost always when I ask people why they wish to enter spiritual direction, their answer has something to do with prayer. 'I need help in prayer. I want to deepen my prayer life. I want to learn to pray better.' They feel they do not pray enough and want at least to be scolded or excused for their deficiencies. More important is the sense that they are somehow not praying correctly. Implicit is the expectation that there is a right way or a secret recipe, something that can be taught to them cognitively.

While that consummate teacher of prayer, the author of *The Cloud* and *The Book of Privy Counselling*, is making a strong case for what we know as Centring Prayer, he seems also to be acknowledging that there are different temperaments and needs, hence there is no single right way to pray:

> Do not pray with words unless you are really drawn to this; or if you do pray with words, pay no attention to whether they are many or few. Do not weigh them in their meaning. Do not be concerned about what kind of prayers you use, for it is unimportant whether or not they are official liturgical prayers, psalms, hymns, or anthems; whether they are

for particular or general intentions; or whether you formulate them interiorly, by thoughts, or express them aloud, in words.[31]

Essential only is that there be 'a naked intent stretching out towards God'.

These are good precepts to be borne in mind by the spiritual director as a teacher of prayer. I have to be careful not to try to impose my own image on the directee. What is right for me at the moment may not be right for the directee; there is often the temptation, especially when our own prayer is going well, to prescribe our present way to everyone.

For the timid and unsure, those who feel uncertain of their right to address God, the model of Jesus as a teacher of prayer is important. Repeatedly the gospels depict him as going apart to pray and as praying silently in the presence of others. Had it been possible to listen in, the disciples need not have asked, 'Lord, teach us to pray' (Luke 11:1). His response is direct and revelatory of his own intimate relationship with God the Father. In his gift of the Our Father, he invites his disciples to partake of this intimacy. Moreover he urges candour and persistence: keep asking, keep knocking on the door. I find that directees are often unacquainted with the verses which follow immediately upon the Our Father and therefore assume that vigorous prayers of petition are somehow not nice and are to be repressed. It is a surprise to them to read the story of the man who keeps knocking on his friend's door at midnight until he gets want he wants.[32] In a similar vein is the parable of the widow who pesters the judge until he decides in her favour.[33] Is it really all right to pray like this? To make a nuisance of oneself, to have bad manners, to **nag**? It is, and our directees need to be assured that they are in good – if not always polite – company if they pray from the heart.

Books on prayer can be helpful, but should be prescribed cautiously, first of all because it is possible to substitute reading **about** prayer for the prayer itself. Further, most directees will obediently read and try to adopt what we suggest, even if it is not suitable. Worse still, they may **not** follow the suggestion, then feel guilty at their own 'disobedience'. So the feeling of inadequacy and failure is increased rather than mitigated.

[31] *The Cloud*, p. 149.
[32] Luke 11:5–13.
[33] Luke 18:1–8.

There is always a task of discernment for the director: should the directee be encouraged to persevere with his present way of praying, even though it may feel stale and difficult, or is it time for a radically new approach? This has to be done on a case-by-case basis: sometimes seeming fruitlessness is a sign that breakthrough is about to happen, and sometimes it is a sign that the directee is persisting in outgrown ways, hence needs to be encouraged to stretch, grow and take risks.

There are times when less is more. Spiritual gluttony can be very real, especially if the person comes to spiritual direction from a recent conversion experience or is addicted to what my English friend Janet calls 'little books'. Filling one's shelves with books about prayer is a poor substitute for prayer itself, and immersing oneself in other people's recipes for the spiritual life is an effective delaying tactic for avoiding necessary inner work. Then the prescription of faithfulness and simplicity is in order. One of our recent seminary graduates assures me that I once told her to stay out of chapel for a while after she confided in me that her over-conscientious attendance at community services was causing her own rich life of contemplative prayer to dry up. Indeed I must have so advised, knowing her to be a person of great spiritual depth and faithfulness. (She assures me that going on a diet was just what she needed and that within a short time she was back in the seminary chapel – not, however, feeling compelled to be there every time the bell rang.)

I prefer to work with suggestions rather than specific assignments. 'You might try this' or 'This has been helpful to me' is usually enough to open the way for new approaches. As noted above, the proximity of **pray** and **play** is too striking to be overlooked. The directee can be encouraged to explore her images for God. This is especially liberating for women (and men) who find the accepted liturgical language overwhelmingly patriarchal. It may take a while to convince them that, in solitary prayer, they are free to find their own images and terms of address for God and that they are indeed in excellent company. (One need think only of Julian's 'Jesus our mother' and Teresa of Avila's 'Majesty'.)

For directees who claim they never have time to pray, we can encourage them to find new places and occasions. Two of my favourite holy places are the underground and the kitchen. Both could be seen as spiritually empty or wasted spaces, something to be got through as quickly as possible so that real living can be resumed. However, I find that the underground – where the sight of the wounded Body of Christ is inescapable – is a fruitful place for prayers of intercession, while repetitive tasks in the kitchen can be sanctified by the Jesus Prayer. Directees can be encouraged to pray while walking or before opening a book in the library or while performing manual labour. One colleague tells me that he combines centring prayer with his daily half-hour of running.

There are so many avenues – praying imaginatively in the Ignatian way or following the author of *The Cloud* in imageless prayer; praying with the aid of icons, crucifixes, candles and rosaries; praying standing, sitting, kneeling and prostrate; praying through writing a journal; praying the Jesus Prayer of the heart; letting scripture speak to us through the method of *lectio divina*. It is a rich feast, and it is important for the director to be sparing with suggestions. Too much at once is an excessively lavish buffet. Spiritual indigestion is as real as spiritual gluttony.

The spiritual director can help people be truly themselves, to (paraphrasing Merton) define themselves authentically and spontaneously in relation to God. In other words, she can help them to pray.

Shaping a rule

People also come to spiritual direction seeking aid in formulating a rule of life. While some, particularly those attracted to the customs of monasticism, articulate this clearly in traditional religious terms, the desire for help in shaping and structuring the daily routine is implicit in almost every case.

As commonly conceived, most rules are quasi-monastic, dealing chiefly with allotment and nature of prayer time; liturgical observance, that is, the frequency of attendance at the Eucharist and perhaps the regular reception of the sacrament of reconciliation; and some form of accountability, such as letters at stated intervals to a designated member of the religious order (if one is an associate), ongoing meetings with a Cursillo group, or periodic meetings with a spiritual director. In other words, what is the pattern of the specifically 'religious' parts of one's life? Henry, for example, arrives in my office with a concise, tidy list: he will be present at the Eucharist on Sunday, spend twenty minutes a day in centring prayer, make an annual three-day retreat at a nearby convent, and make his confession in Advent and Lent. He isn't really asking for my help in forming his rule; he just wants my approval. It's a good enough rule, in a traditional sense, for it provides an intentional basis for a life lived in awareness of God.

But a good rule goes beyond the narrowly devotional. If we are to be whole people, it must be more than a schedule for our visiting hours with God. I can tell by looking at Henry that he doesn't get any exercise, and I remember his discomfort at the lack of ash trays in my office. Yet he has left no place in his rule for care and restoration of his body. I know too, from our conversations, that his marriage has become grim and silent. I'm delighted at his plan to spend three days in the convent, but feel impelled to suggest he devotes a similar long weekend to his wife, away from household cares, in the best resort hotel he can afford.

There is a common tendency to try to take on too much, to try to live a monastic life amidst the stimuli and pressures of the everyday late-twentieth-century world. Instead of retreating to a quiet oratory for morning prayer, many people begin their day with an hour on the motorway or public transport. Can the rule of life be adapted to turn a commute into a place and time of prayer? How does one manage extended periods of contemplative prayer when there is a new baby in the house, and perhaps a few toddlers underfoot as well? Not easily! A rule of life for people living in families, where each member is at a different place spiritually, calls for creativity and flexibility. And most of us live with the absence of community support; it is a painful fact that seriously observant Christians are in the minority in our society. Hence most of our associates in the workplace and the neighbourhood may follow the civil religion – of the left or the right – but can scarcely say with the Psalmist, 'zeal for thy house has consumed me'.[34] Further, how can a rule help us deal with the anxieties endemic to our place and time, to see the God-connection in the seemingly godless afflictions of illness, unemployment, violence and fear?

Someone once likened a rule of life to a rose trellis. Its purpose is to support, to set us free from the tyranny of 'shoulds' and 'oughts', in other words to set us free for growth. As such, it is an instrument to be used and adapted, rather than a monument carved in stone.

A good rule deals with traditional matters of devotional practice, but goes further to encompass the stewardship of energy,

[34] Psalm 69:9.

creativity, and especially time. We are a time-obsessed people in a way unthinkable to the author of *The Cloud*, who cautions:

> Be attentive to time and the way you spend it. Nothing is more precious. This is evident when you recall that in one tiny moment heaven may be gained or lost. God, the master of time, never gives the future. He gives only the present, moment by moment. . . Man will not be able to excuse himself at the last judgment, saying to God: 'You overwhelmed me with the future when I was only capable of living in the present.'[35]

Most of the people who come to us for direction value their time, protest vigorously that they do not have enough of it, and would probably deny that they waste it. Yet the commandment to observe the Sabbath is routinely – and even proudly – violated by many of us who are meticulous (or at least semi-conscious) in our observance of the other nine. 'Not wasting time' becomes an excuse for neglecting time for true rest and reflection, what the poet Lessing called 'the creative pause'. Most important, we can use busyness and crowded schedules to hide from God. Even as we delude ourselves that we are being good stewards, we fill our days so tightly that we close him out. Our excessive busyness masks the sin of sloth.

As directors we work with time-conscious men and women who may already feel guilty about not having time to pray. While they may be responsible stewards of their substance, they need a workable rule of life to bring proportion to their stewardship of time and energy.

I sometimes ask people to keep a careful record of their activities, hour by hour, for a day – and better still, for a week. This is analogous to the helpful practice of dieting for weight loss, in which the dieter records each morsel of food taken in. In both cases there are surprises. The person who 'eats nothing' discovers she has been eating all day, taking in a highly calorific mouthful here, a highly calorific mouthful there. The person who would like to pray but 'has no time' may find that he is able to watch reruns of *The Odd Couple* and never misses *Twin Peaks* (or whatever the current media fad may be). But it is not fair of me to single out television, although its influence is insidious; late-twentieth-century citizens have almost unlimi-

---

[35] *The Cloud*, pp. 50–1.

ted opportunities for consumption, stimulation and empty activity.

At any rate, when the log of activity is examined, it will reveal soft places, waste and evasions. The directee is able to see time as a precious gift, to be used and structured. Then it is time to create a rule which takes into account the relationship to God, others and one's deepest self. Areas of disproportion and hence potential sinfulness become apparent, so that the rule can serve as a reminder where caution is needed. Self-care is a holy obligation; yet a surprising number of people formulate a rule which stipulates how many minutes a day will be spent in prayer or how many times a week they will be present at the Eucharist, but ignore their dangerous addictions to food, alcohol or nicotine. Finally there needs to be provision for sheer fun. It was a joyous insight when I realised that in Middle English 'silly' meant 'blessed', cognate with the Modern German *selig*. So I find myself asking directees, 'What have you put in this rule for fun? Where's the blessed silliness in it?' The outward form of the rule is not important: it can be a terse outline of a few words, or it can run to several pages to be included in a journal. It is, after all, a quite disposable document, subject always to review and revision.

Homework?

I have already noted my reluctance to **assign** readings. The directee may dutifully plough through the book, looking in vain for its application to her own situation; or, for whatever reason, she will not attempt it. In either case I have added a burden and increased the risk of dependency in the relationship, that is, it becomes more important to please the director or at least avoid her displeasure than to discover together what is pleasing to God. Further, all too many people already live in their heads and use the cognitive as a way of avoiding the experience of God. There is nothing wrong with suggesting titles that will help them be better informed scripturally, theologically or historically, as long as both of us are clear about what we are doing, and do not let the spiritual direction meetings turn into an enquirer's class. Directees who are intellectually hungry can be encouraged to participate more fully in their parish's education programme or urged to take a course in the diocesan school of theology. Most seminaries welcome part-time students, and denominational lines can be easily crossed.

While I rarely assign, I frequently suggest: 'This book spoke to me; you might find it helpful too. But don't feel you have to stick with it if it doesn't feel right.' It is important that the suggestion be offered very lightly and then dropped. Sometimes it bears fruit slowly. A directee recently came to my study, full of enthusiasm about a book I had mentioned over a year ago. She confessed that she had stopped to buy it at the seminary bookshop on her way home, looked at it briefly and, finding it almost incomprehensible, put it on the shelf. A year later she took it down and discovered that it was just what she needed. Her timing was better than mine!

I always encourage people to read the Bible, not beginning with Genesis and ending with the almost inevitable breakdown in Leviticus or – for the truly tenacious – in Chronicles. Rather, I invite them to begin with one of the gospels and to read it through as if it were a long-awaited bestseller. This shocks the pious, who heretofore have read scripture 'devotionally', that is, with their minds turned off and their emotions deadened. But it also awakens them to the vitality of the Bible and the connection of their own story with that of the gospel. Next I suggest Psalms, pointing out that while the 23rd offers familiar comfort, Psalm 88:6–7 might be more realistic for certain moods:

> You have laid me in the depths of the Pit,
>   In dark places, and in the abyss.
> Your anger weighs upon me heavily,
>   and all your great waves overwhelm me.
> You have put my friends far from me;
>   you have made me to be abhorred by them;
>   I am in prison and cannot get free.

For those who have trouble acknowledging their own anger, the extravagant vengefulness of Psalm 58:6–8 is an eye-opener:

> O God, break their [the enemies'] teeth in their mouths;
>   pull the fangs of the young lions, O LORD.
> Let them vanish like water that runs off;
>   Let them wither like the trodden grass.
> Let them be like the snail that melts away,
>   like a stillborn child that never sees the sun.

It is vastly freeing for directees to become aware of the range of human emotion in the Psalms, often a liberating surprise for those who are fearful of expressing doubt, despair or rage.

It is informative to ask what the directee has been reading. Particularly in the early stages of the relationship, it is possible to learn some of the questions which he is not yet able to articulate. Sometimes I discover that the directee has set himself a nearly impossible or unsuitable task. For example, David – an absolute newcomer to Christianity – was struggling through Dom Gregory Dix's *Shape of the Liturgy*, a work of immense historic value but overwhelming to a beginner. I suggested he became more familiar with the Prayer Book itself, as a first step.

There are other kinds of assignments that form a bridge between our meetings. I have already noted the importance of encouraging the directee to explore new ways, times and places of praying, especially when the present practices have become perfunctory. Frequently my assignment is to 'lighten up', not to turn prayer into a work but to listen for God and let oneself be surprised. Overly rigid adherence to a spiritual discipline built around formal liturgical observance and highly structured prayer-time can work against the sanctification of the ordinary. Christ is effectively imprisoned, to be visited at stated times and otherwise ignored. So I might suggest listening for God during a walk in a dirty city street, in the quiet of the country, or perhaps for a few minutes when cuddling an infant or a child. (It is a blessing to work at the General Theological Seminary, where infants and small children are always available on loan!)

In our tendency to spiritualise we neglect our bodies. Particularly in my work with seminarians, I find myself enquiring about nutrition, exercise and sleep habits and bordering on the authoritarian in discussions of self-care. Directees limited by chronic or debilitating illness need to be reminded that driving themselves to the limit of endurance is destructive, not heroic. Arthur, who suffers from a degenerative disease and whose prognosis is poor, needs help in overcoming denial of his condition. He sees his illness as a divinely sent test (if not an affliction) and is determined to carry on as if it did not exist. It is hard for him to ask for help and even harder to care for himself when his coordination fails and his body cries out for rest. He berates himself for unfaithfulness when an episode of ill health forces him to curtail, even temporarily, his volunteer work in a shelter for the homeless. It is hard work to lead him to love his own ailing body as much as he loves the guests at the shelter.

A certain bossiness on my part regarding self-care seems to

be welcome, as if the directee were saying to himself, 'If my spiritual director says I must, then I really must go for a run or play a game of tennis. And it's a matter of holy obedience to get a sitter at least twice a month so that I can spend an evening alone with my wife.' There is a certain playful complicity: the directee and I both know that the 'assignment' is really a permission, a permission which wouldn't be necessary if he were able to honour and care for himself as a part of Creation.

Most frequently my assignments are to 'think about' something. I invite the directee to think about her images of God, God's possible images for her, the stepping stones or turning points in her life, the lovely or not so lovely skins she may have shed at each point of transformation. I urge people to make a list or at least notes, not because written work must be turned in and evaluated, but because writing fosters focus and specificity. I have to work hard to remember that some people find writing a burden so that the mere suggestion of keeping a journal constricts the flow of thought and images. So I urge them to find their own way here – perhaps writing in a beautifully bound little book with a proper fountain pen, perhaps using a word processor, maybe even a tape recorder.

Finally I ask directees to be attentive to causes for celebration in their lives. This can be hard work, especially when they feel they are abandoned by God and living at the bottom of a pit. Some gentle humour helps there, as does the memory of Corrie ten Boom. The devout Dutchwoman and her sister Betsie were attempting to obey Paul's injunction to the Thessalonians to give thanks for all things, even the circumstances of their imprisonment in the Nazi concentration camp at Ravensbruck.

> 'Thank you,' Betsie went on serenely, 'for the fleas and for –'
>
> The fleas! That was too much. 'Betsie, there's no way even God can make me grateful for a flea.'
>
> ' "Give thanks in *all* circumstances",' she quoted. 'It doesn't say, "in pleasant circumstances". Fleas are part of this place where God has put us.'[36]

Later the sisters discovered why they and the other women had been relatively free of harassment from the camp guards in that barrack-room: it was crawling with fleas, and the guards feared contagion.

[36] Corrie ten Boom, *The Hiding Place*, pp. 198–9.

It should be clear that our directees are not expected to live up to Corrie's heroic sanctity, nor should we encourage them to seek and enjoy suffering. But almost everyone is tormented by some version of Corrie's fleas. Indeed, spiritual fleas may be much harder to bear than more spectacular ills. The little nuisances lose their power, however, if – lightly, ironically, even with chagrin – we and our directees can give thanks for them as 'part of the place where God has put us'.

The slow work of God

> Some brothers ... went to see Abba Felix and they begged him to say a word to them. But the old man kept silence. After they had asked him for a long time he said to them 'You wish to hear a word?' They said, 'Yes, abba.' Then the old man said to them, 'There are no more words nowadays.'[37]

It is only human to want to be wise and to say the right thing. Especially when people come to us for spiritual direction, we usually assume that – like the abba's disciples – they expect something profound, even life-changing, from us. But spiritual directors, like all good teachers, need to live with the silence, not just to endure it but to be comfortable with it. If we are to assist people in the work of knowing and being known, to define themselves authentically and spontaneously in relation to God and their world, then we must be willing to wait with them and often to acknowledge that there are no words.

This means an acceptance of plateaux, of periods when there seems to be no progress. In a culture that is production- and task-orientated, the director-teacher celebrates open-endedness. Even when the directee accepts the possibility of transformation (which is always behind the seeking out of a director), she may nevertheless be unwilling or unable to accept the discomfort of waiting when there are no words.

Silence is rarely comfortable. We are acculturated to wanting certainty and clarity. Yet in the silence we embrace ambiguity and darkness. People who come for spiritual direction often want answers, want even to be told what to do. But if they persevere they discover that the darkness and silence increase rather than decrease. (After all, according to the tradition, the 'dark night of the soul' – characterised by a painful sense of the

[37] Benedicta Ward, p. 242.

absence of God – is an advanced state achieved by relatively few.) The author of *The Cloud* adjures us to

> learn to be at home in this darkness. Return to it as often as you can, letting your spirit cry out to him whom you love. For if, in this life, you hope to feel and see God as he is in himself it must be within this darkness and this cloud.[38]

People who come to spiritual direction seeking answers find that, instead, their questions proliferate. The great central question remains: 'Good teacher, what must I do to inherit eternal life?' Yet as they explore it, moving towards its heart, the mystery deepens. Spiritual directors do well to recall Rilke's advice to the young poet: to love and to live the questions.

Good teachers love questions because, with Rilke, they love the mystery of locked rooms and books that are written in a very foreign tongue. With Teilhard de Chardin, they understand the need for almost infinite patience and trust:

> Above all, trust in the slow work of God,
> We are, quite naturally,
> impatient in everything to reach the end
> without delay.
> We should like to skip
> the intermediate stages.
> We are impatient of being
> on the way to something unknown,
> something new,
> And yet it is the law of all progress
> that it is made by passing through
> some stages of instability –
> And that it may take a very long time.
>
> And so I think it is with you.
> Your ideas mature gradually –
> let them grow,
> let them shape themselves,
> without undue haste.
> Don't try to force them on,
> as though you could be today
> what time (that is to say, grace and
> circumstances acting

---

[38] *The Cloud*, p. 49.

on your own good will)
will make you tomorrow.

Only God could say what this new spirit
gradually forming within you will be.
Give our Lord the benefit of believing
that his hand is leading you,

and accept the anxiety of
feeling yourself in suspense and incomplete.[39]

---

[39] I am indebted to the Revd Elizabeth Canham, Obl. OHC, for acquainting
me with this poem by Teilhard.

3

THE SPIRITUAL DIRECTOR AS MIDWIFE

Once it appeared to a person as if in a dream – it was a daydream – as if he were pregnant with nothing as a woman is pregnant with a child. And God was born in this nothing: he was the fruit of nothing. God was born in nothing. (Meister Eckhart)[1]

In the soul that abides in a present now, God begets his only begotten son, and in this birth the soul is born again in God. It is one birth: as often as the soul is born in God, the Father begets his only begotten Son in the soul. (Meister Eckhart)[2]

Tend only to the birth in you and you will find all goodness and all consolation, all delight, all being and all truth. Reject it and you reject goodness and blessing. What comes to you in this birth brings with it pure being and blessing. But what you seek or love outside of this birth will come to nothing, no matter what you will or where you will it. (Meister Eckhart)[3]

This man came to Jesus by night and said to him, 'Rabbi, we know that you are a teacher come from God; for no one can do these signs that you do, unless God is with him. Jesus answered him, 'Truly, truly, I say to you, unless one is born anew, he cannot see the kingdom of God.' Nicodemus said to him, 'How can a man be born when he is old? Can he enter a second time into his mother's womb and be born?' (John 3:2–4)

[1] *'Surrexit autem Saulus de Terra'*, no. 37 in *Deutsche Predigten*, ed. Joseph Quint, p. 332.
[2] *'Ubi est, qui natus est'*, no. 57 in ibid. p. 426.
[3] Ibid. p. 425.

Then the king of Egypt said to the Hebrew midwives, one of whom was named Shiphrah and the other Puah, 'When you serve as midwife to the Hebrew women, and see them upon the birthstool, if it is a son, you shall kill him; but if it is a daughter, she shall live.' But the midwives feared God, and did not do as the king of Egypt commanded them, but let the male children live. So the king of Egypt called the midwives, and said to them, 'Why have you done this, and let the male children live?' The midwives said to Pharaoh, 'Because the Hebrew women are not like the Egyptian women; for they are vigorous and are delivered before the midwife comes to them.' So God dealt well with the midwives; and the people multiplied and grew very strong. And because the midwives feared God he gave them families.[4]

SHIPHRAH AND PUAH – hardly household names! These two brave, intensely practical women are hidden in the rich narrative of the Exodus, meriting only a few lines of text over against the exhaustive account of Moses' leadership of Israel. To be sure, we are told their names, a relatively rare occurrence in scripture and particularly in the Old Testament, where males (and a patriarchal God) are commonly the initiators of action. But where would the story be without these midwives, tenacious and crafty guardians of new life?

Ironically, Shiphrah and Puah stand guardian of the Exodus story and – ultimately – of **our** story. Our family album is God's word written down by male authors and dealing primarily with male experience. Yet it is punctuated by stories of pregnancy and birth, stories of new life that redirect and transform. Shiphrah and Puah are joined by Hagar who fled into the wilderness with her son; Sarah who laughed at the very idea of motherhood; Rachel who wept for her children; and Hannah whose fervour in prayer for a child was mistaken for drunkenness. These pivotal women of the Old Testament prepare us for **the** story, the great mystery of the incarnation, made immediate and vivid in Luke's sensitive telling. Any woman who has carried a child within her has echoed Mary's 'How can this be?' even as she has experienced Mary's joy, fear and bafflement, her need for solitude and for companionship.

With the fact of the incarnation at the centre of our faith, it is not surprising that our language of piety is filled with the

[4]Exodus 1:15–21.

imagery of birthgiving. So Paul, that reputed misogynist, describes the yearning for God in terms of the first stage of labour:

> Up to the present, we know, the whole created universe groans in all its parts as if in the pangs of childbirth. Not only so, but even we, to whom the Spirit is given as first-fruits of the harvest to come, are groaning inwardly while we wait for God to make us his sons [and daughters] and set our whole body free.[5]

I'm not sure how, but he seems to know what he is talking about, that birth is a difficult, painful and messy process.

Most powerful is John's account of Jesus' conversation with Nicodemus the Pharisee, who came to him by night, secretly and drawn by mystery. Jesus answers his question before he can ask it, telling the seeker perhaps more than he wants to know: you must be born anew. There is irony and humour in this story as two learned men discuss the logistics of birth, how to repeat a seemingly unrepeatable experience. Nicodemus, like Mary, exclaims in wonderment, 'How can this be?'

Then there is the Psalmist's powerful image of YHWH as midwife:

Yet you are he who took me out of the womb, and kept me safe
    upon my mother's breast.
I have been entrusted to you ever since I was born; you were
    my God when I was still in my mother's womb.[6]

Set as they are in Psalm 22, that great cry of desolation and abandonment, these verses are especially poignant. We are reminded that the midwife helps new life into being and pro-tects it; even more than the mother, she is the tender guardian of its safety.

Despite decades of reading this Psalm and hearing it read solemnly each Maundy Thursday, I had passed over its com-pelling picture of God as birth-helper until one day the words leaped at me from the page. Shiphrah and Puah may well stand as our icon, the foremothers of all midwives, but behind them is another faithful guardian of new life. The Lord is my

[5]Romans 8:22–23.
[6]Psalm 22:9–10.

shepherd, I shall not want. The Lord is also my midwife; I shall be kept safe.

The maternal and birth imagery of scripture along with the stories of births miraculous and ordinary have become so much a part of our religious consciousness that they threaten to recede into the background, to become a kind of neutral spiritual wallpaper. To be 'born again' has a charismatic, quite disembodied ring to it; to some mainline Christians, and certainly to many Anglicans, it smacks of an emotional excess. The Annunciation, too, has become disembodied, transformed by artists – from Memling to the unnamed crafters of Christmas cards – into a beautiful tableau instead of a terrifying encounter. It helps purge the scene of sentimental piety if one is able to imagine it occurring in the ordinariness of daily life.

Yet these and other stories of birth and birthing are not mere background. Rather, they form the rich matrix of our faith. From them life pulses through the most patriarchal pages of the Bible.

One of the liberating effects of the women's movement has been to make a large body of human experience available, acceptable and usable. Just as Bertolt Brecht revolutionised the theatre by presenting the ordinary as if it were extraordinary, so our present broadened perspective permits us new ways of seeing and of making connections. It is all too easy to see the birth imagery in scripture (and in the language of popular piety) as abstract, bloodless, remote from human experience. Yet if I were to name my own most profound spiritual or theological experience, without hesitation I would cite the birth of my three children. This has nothing to do with my fondness for babies *per se* – like everyone else they can be charming or difficult, attractive or not – nor with my personal (and biased) relationship with my own children. Rather, each birth was a gift, a glimpse into the mystery of Creation and incarnation.

It is time that, with Eckhart, we tend to the birth in us. Some of us have given birth; others have witnessed or assisted in bringing new life into the world. Certainly, all have read books, seen movies and listened to stories; all of us have our baggage of fears, revulsion, envy, fascination – and not necessarily in that order. Most important, we have all been born. We all began in the dark shelter of the womb and moved into the light. And even though we may die alone, no one was born alone. To be born presupposes relationship, connection, community.

Even as we are born in the human birth process, so we are

born again in our baptism. And if Eckhart is to be believed, we
give birth and are born again and again: the birth of God in the
soul is our own true birth. Like the Hebrew women in Egypt,
we need help. We need midwives, those careful assistants with
whom God deals well.

The idea of the spiritual director as midwife appeals to me,
personally and emotionally. I am not drawn to the Socratic
model, for his midwives were sterile. Moreover they were
people of acknowledged power, controlling the process of
birth and judging the worthiness of the new life to survive:

> No woman .. who is still able to conceive and bear,
> attends to other women, but only those who are past
> bearing. . . And by the use of potions and incantations they
> are able to arouse the pangs and to soothe them at will,
> and, if they think fit, they can smother the embryo in the
> womb.[7]

There is a cold, hard edge to these Socratic midwives! I would
rather emulate Shiphrah and Puah in their courage and commitment.

Or I might model my spiritual midwife on the Celtic knee-
woman or aid-woman, making birth a sacrament. As described
by Alexander Carmichael in his *Carmina Gadelica*, the newborn
would be handed across the fire three times, then carried sun-
wise around the fire three times. Then the midwife continued
the ritual:

> When the image of the God of life is born into the world I
> put three little drops of water on the child's forehead. I
> put the first little drop in the name of the Father, and the
> watching-women say Amen. I put the second little drop in
> the name of the Son, and the watching-women say Amen.
> I put the third little drop in the name of the Spirit, and
> the watching-women say Amen. And I beseech the Holy
> Three to lave and bathe the child and to preserve it in
> Themselves. And the watching-women say Amen. All the
> people in the house are raising their voices with the
> watching-women, giving witness that the child has been
> committed to the blessed Trinity. By the Book itself! ear
> has never heard music more beautiful than the music of

[7]'Theaetetus', in *The Dialogues of Plato*, tr. B. Jowett (London: Oxford University Press 1953), Vol. 3, pp. 243–4.

the watching-women when they are consecrating the seed of man and committing him to the great God of life.[8]

This was the 'birth baptism'; the child would be formally baptised eight days later.

Most of all I am attracted to the Appalachian granny-woman of earlier days, willing to travel by foot or by mule over the rough terrain of the southern mountains to be present at remote and humble nativities. She lives on in oral tradition, but her image is fading. I picture her as unflappable, filled with a tough compassion and able to make do with whatever might be at hand. A spiritual granny-woman is ready for anything!

It is important to remember that the midwife is not necessarily a wife, or even a woman. The literal meaning of the word is 'with-woman', that is, the person who is with the birthgiver. Until recent times (and still, in other parts of the world), women gave birth with the assistance of another woman whose expertise was based on her own experience of giving birth. During the nineteenth and twentieth centuries the practice fell out of fashion and was even legally suppressed in the so-called developed countries; but midwifery is now enjoying a resurgence. The new breed is neither knee-women nor granny-women, but highly trained health professionals.

Like the midwife, spiritual directors are with-women and with-men. While biological birthgiving is the prerogative of the female and while midwives are traditionally female, in the ministry of spiritual direction anatomy is not destiny. Accordingly the feminine imagery and language of this chapter do not imply exclusivity. Both men and women can be sensitive midwives of the soul.

What the midwife does[9]

The midwife is present to another in a time of vulnerability, working in areas that are deep and intimate. It is a relationship of trust and mutual respect. Unlike most physicians, she does

[8] Quoted in *The Celtic Vision*, ed. Esther de Waal (London, DLT 1988; Petersham, Mass: St Bede's Publications 1988), p. 111. A similar prayer is recorded by Avery Brooke in *Celtic Prayers* (London and NY, Seabury Press 1981), pp. 22–7.

[9] For the information that follows I am indebted to Barbara Brennan and Joan Rattner Heilman for *The Complete Book of Midwifery*, with a grateful nod to Eckhart, who says nothing about midwifery but a great deal about birth.

not fear that her professionalism will be threatened by a degree of intimacy with the women who have come to her for help. She is willing to be called by her given name, even as she addresses the birthgiver by **hers**. She does things **with**, not **to** the person giving birth.

The midwife is also a teacher in the best sense of the word, in that she helps the birthgiver towards ever greater self-knowledge. From the very beginning she takes time to establish a comfortable relationship, one in which no question is irrelevant or 'stupid'. As the authors of *The Complete Book of Midwifery* note, 'Almost every patient we've ever had in our service has told us that they've felt so much more comfortable and free to be themselves with us. They are not embarrassed to ask personal questions, to expose their fears and their bodies.'[10] The midwife invites questions and then takes time to answer them: 'We don't sit behind a desk and shuffle papers as we ask if a patient has any questions. We always sit down next to her and talk as long as she wants, especially during the early pre-natal visits when she's usually bursting with questions.'[11]

The midwife assists at a natural event. Unlike the physician, she does not deal with sickness or pathology, but she is knowledgeable enough to seek help when these are present. She does not rely on heavy dosages of drugs to cover pain and dull memory. Traditionally she uses her hands rather than instruments or tools. She uses them to wipe sweat from a forehead; to hold the birthgiver's hand; and finally to guide, steady and receive the baby. Under her guidance the birthing is a human process, based on human and humane contact throughout.

She sees clearly what the birthgiver cannot see. She knows the transition period – a time of desolation, of seemingly unmanageable pain and nausea – to be a sign of breakthrough and great progress. She can encourage and interpret when the birthgiver may feel that she has lost control and failed. She knows when the birthgiver should push, when she should hold back, when she should breathe deeply, and when to pant in shallow breaths. The mother's body **should** know this instinctively, but fear and pain may cause her to forget.

The midwife knows how and when to confront. The art of confrontation is a delicate one, sometimes mistakenly confused with clumsy attack. To confront is quite literally to face

[10] Ibid. p. 57.
[11] Ibid. p. 61.

another; in midwifery, both physical and spiritual, the helper's loving detachment can bring clarity to the situation. Sometimes it is a simple acknowledgement of the intensity of pain: 'Don't be afraid to complain, even to scream. Don't be afraid to ask for relief.' At other times it is a gentle reminder that the birthgiver is still in control and has the power to help herself; so perhaps screaming is an over-dramatic and self-indulgent reaction at this point. Like a good coach or teacher or leader in combat, the midwife is able to give heart, to ask and even demand the seemingly impossible.

And finally the midwife rejoices in the baby. With the birthgiver, she is able to celebrate the beauty and absurdity of the tiny new creature.

Some of the facts of life, physical and spiritual

When I began to do the work of spiritual direction, that is, to assist at the spiritual birthgiving of others, I was struck by the similarities to the physical birth process. For those who have not experienced it first-hand, it would be good to know what we are talking about. So the paragraphs which follow weave together a brief sketch of the progress of pregnancy and birth along with the analogous spiritual process. (As I remind my students at the seminary, an old Red Cross film might serve the purpose equally well.)

First there is a **long period of waiting and uncertainty**. The birthgiver thinks: maybe I'm not even pregnant, but somehow I feel different. Very different! The range of experiences and feelings during this time is staggering – joy mingles with sadness, eager expectancy with unaccustomed drowsiness. For some there is nausea, and for nearly everyone there is the phenomenon of changing tastes. All the stale jokes about pickles and ice cream have their basis in human experience. It feels as if everything is changing, and emotions become extreme and unreliable. Almost simultaneously the pregnant woman feels powerlessness and great power, hope for the future and fear of the unknown. Extroverts become introspective and amaze themselves in their bovine placidity. In time, the sense of distortion becomes physical as well as emotional: the body looks simply **wrong**, out of shape and uncomfortably tight around the waist – at least until the pregnancy is sufficiently advanced for the proud strut of visible fecundity. And there is growing physical clumsiness – something has happened to the sense of balance!

This is a minimum list. Every time I play this game with other spiritual directors or with seminarians who are biological mothers, we are able to add to it from our collective experience. And it is striking how often the same 'symptoms' are displayed by those who come – tentatively or aggressively – seeking spiritual direction.

How does a woman know she is pregnant with a child? How do you know you are spiritually pregnant? When – on perhaps a very modest scale – the angel has come to you from the pages of scripture, in the liturgy, in the consciousness of study or the unconsciousness of dreams? When the angel has come to you in a flash of awareness, often in a highly 'unspiritual' setting – the office, the supermarket, your car on the motorway – and said, 'Hail, O favoured one, have I got a deal for you! Get ready to have your life turned upside down.'

In both cases, time will tell. In physical pregnancy the early signs can be deceptive, particularly for the inexperienced. Decades ago, for two months I attributed mysterious and altered feelings to Mexico City's high altitude and assumed that I would 'adjust'. Time told differently! Similarly in later stages of pregnancy, the first flutter of new life can be dismissed as a delusion, a trick of the imagination. It simply does not seem earth-shaking enough. In the same way the initial stirrings of the Spirit within us may be small and homely, easily discounted because they do not seem earth-shaking.

While the symptoms of spiritual malaise and imbalance bear careful attention, not everyone is pregnant, that is, not everyone is a candidate for direction, at least not at every stage of life. There are those who are religiously observant and content with their spiritual lives as part of a worshipping community. It would not occur to them to enter into the intense, one-to-one relationship of traditional direction, nor even to become part of a 'spiritual friends' group. This is perhaps a matter of temperament as well as generation and life experience. Then there are those whose spirituality is directed outwards. They encounter God in service, in action, in outreach. Spiritual rhythms are like bodily rhythms: respiration requires both inhaling and exhaling, taking in and letting go. Frequently, but not always, those who are turning outwards – exhaling, as it were – are not in the right place for spiritual direction. Later, perhaps, but not at the moment.

But there are those who feel that something is happening to and within them. Their tastes are changing and their balance has shifted. Sometimes they are brought up short by a crisis: an experience of conversion, a tragic loss, a period of great pain, a sharp awareness of being on a threshold. As they approach mid-life women, especially, may feel impelled to explore their spirituality as they discover their new and unexpectedly authoritative voice. Men and women of all ages and life experience may sense a call, not necessarily a vocation to the ordained ministry, but simply the awareness that God expects them to do something with their lives. What? Sometimes they merely experience a pervasive but indefinable spiritual dis-ease which has nothing to do with pathology, but aches and itches until help is sought. Sometimes they come filled with surprise and joy: after years, perhaps decades, of faithful observance, they have experienced a sudden awareness of God's presence and grace. They feel fruitful, joyous, and expectant – and don't know what to do about it.

As a spiritual midwife, the director's task is to pay attention, to listen to what is not being said (or to what is being said but minimised). Those seeking a spiritual director for the first time are almost invariably apologetic and quick to minimise their experience of Annunciation, at least until they are reassured of its validity. So our conversations often begin with a disclaimer: 'I'm not really sure why I'm here. I shouldn't be taking up your time. But. . .' Talking about God is difficult for mainline Christians of the late-twentieth-century West, and many of those yearning for spiritual direction lack the vocabulary to describe their symptoms and – alas! – the imagination to envision the fruit of their travail. They just know that they are experiencing inner changes, sometimes alarmingly joyful and sometimes profoundly disturbing. Spiritual distortion, imbalance and nausea are no more pleasant than the analogous physical phenomena, even when they are signs of life and fruitfulness.

When in doubt I always assume that God is at work, that is, the person is pregnant. It cannot be said too often: first of all, we must take each person seriously and value that person as a child of God. Just as the good host observes Benedict's admonition that each guest is to be received as if she were Christ himself, so the good midwife assumes that new life is germinating in the person who has sought him out.

After the long time of waiting comes the **onset of labour**.

Like conversion, this can be sudden or slow and gradual. There may be some false alarms. But swift or gradual, tentative or definite, when it finally happens there is a sense of the inevitable. There is no going back, no return to one's original state. This can be simultaneously frightening – matters are out of hand – and joyous – something is **finally** happening.

A ministry of presence, patience and waiting

Then comes **labour itself**. The terminology is apt. Birthing is hard, focused, intense work. Labour is a time of concentration, heightened awareness and attentiveness. But it is not undifferentiated; there are distinct stages, and each must be understood and respected.

The first stage is a time of waiting for the moment of readiness. This is a time of rhythmic contractions, which grow in painful intensity. (Natural childbirth enthusiasts disapprove of designating these as pains, preferring the more upbeat or at least neutral term 'contraction'. But birthgiving, physical or spiritual, is not a totally upbeat process.) Whether this stage is short or long, it is a time of waiting, of letting go, and breathing lightly. Above all it is a time of receptivity and a time for patience (especially on the part of the midwife). This may go against the grain in our impatient, result-orientated society; but effort at this point is counter-productive. Unfortunately we have no stronger word to indicate counter-fruitfulness.

While the initial stages of the direction relationship are obviously a time for story-telling, comparable to the midwife's careful taking of a medical history, much of the work of this stage is also devoted to the story, exploring its depths unhurriedly. It is also a time to explore ways of praying, again in a gentle and unhurried way. The directee who feels stuck in the printed words of the liturgy can be encouraged to pray imaginatively with scripture. The one who simultaneously yearns for and fears solitude might experiment with a retreat at a religious house.

Spiritual direction is not a crisis ministry, even though the initial impulse to seek out a director may arise from a sense of urgent personal need. The spiritual midwife is not an expert called in for the dramatic moments – either a crisis caused by pathology or for the final exciting moment of birth. Like the practical midwife, she works with the whole person and is present throughout the whole process. She 'has time' – unlike the tightly-scheduled physician who is concerned with specifics, complaints and pathology. Or, for that matter, unlike the tightly-scheduled parish clergy, who are concerned with programme, administration and liturgy. She offers support through all stages, even waiting with the birthgiver when 'nothing is happening'. Of course there **are** no times, when 'nothing is happening'. Spiritual growth can be gradual and hidden; the director-midwife can discern or at least trust that something is indeed 'happening'.

As a people, we are not comfortable with waiting. We see it as wasted time and try to avoid it, or at least fill it with trivial busyness. We value action for its own sake. Even in retirement, people are expected to be active and boast that they are 'busier than ever'. It is hard, with Teilhard, to trust in the slow work of God. So the model of pregnancy and birth is a helpful one. Genetic engineers have managed in vitro fertilisation, surrogate pregnancies, and astounding feats with the fecundity of milk cows – but (at least up to now!) they have not managed to speed the process of gestation. There are times when waiting is inevitable, ordained and fruitful.

Along with high valuation of activity *per se*, we believe that we can make things better by our actions. Everything is fixable; and if it isn't broken, it is at least improvable. One need think only of a few of our present idols: pharmacology, medical technology, psychotherapy, and political and economic systems of the right and of the left.

Yet much of spiritual direction is with those who are waiting, who cannot be fixed, repaired, or made right; and the spiritual director does well to emulate the midwife in non-intervention. The midwife understands the process of birthing. In the old days, at least, she had experienced it as well. She knows when she can assist and interpret and when she should merely be present. She intervenes only when necessary and helpful, never for the sake of 'doing something'.

In spiritual directors as in others, the urge to 'help' people dies hard. Even when the director thinks himself purged of such naïvety, the impulse creeps back, often in ever more subtle forms. This is especially true when the directee is in genuine distress and when it is obvious that remediable material or physical circumstances are affecting her spiritual life. People come to us bearing seemingly crushing burdens: chronic illness (both physical and emotional), poverty, the scars of unbelievable abuse. To the director such conditions may seem like adverse ones, to be got rid of or at least tidied up. It is a hard learning that life in Christ is not necessarily a life of pain-free comfort.

I was reminded of this by Jennie. She is isolated, chronically ill, facing ever greater impairment, and living at the edge of poverty. Not long ago as we sat together I found myself thinking, 'If only this woman had a little more money, everything would change. Sure, she would still be ill and lonely, but . . .' I felt myself getting caught in plans to 'help' her, to point out ways of 'fixing everything'. Finally I blurted out, 'I want to take away your pain. I want to be able to make all this go away.' Jennie looked at me with infinite patience, patted my hand, and said, 'Honey, just knowing that you're there and that you love me is enough. Don't worry about it.' She knew what I had forgotten: that sometimes one waits because there is nothing else to be done. The greatest gift I could give her was not to play social worker or psychotherapist, but to quiet down and wait with her. Be with her. To do this, I had to recognise my discomfort at my own powerlessness.

Just as we are not comfortable with waiting, we shrink from passivity, from being the object rather than the initiator of action. The most minor illness can reveal the fragility of our control, as it turns us into **patients**, that is, the recipients of the actions of others, be they healing or hurtful. When we are patients, we have either relinquished control or been deprived of it. Even ascetical theologians would rather talk about it than experience it. We may play a bit at an Eckhartian detachment, letting go of those things or ways of being which are easy to give up, but praying to be spared the cataclysmic experience that rips our carefully woven (or patched) fabric to shreds. Yet the model of holy waiting, of total passivity, is before us in the life of Christ.

In his wise book *The Stature of Waiting*, W. H. Vanstone points out the radical change in Jesus from activity to passivity, noting that the term 'passion' refers not so much to his suffering as to his being done unto, becoming the object rather than the subject. In Mark's gospel, after Judas 'hands him over' (Vanstone prefers this to the more usual translation 'betrays'), he is inactive, speaks very little and then ineffectively. In John's gospel, with the coming of night he becomes inactive; for no work can be done then: it is the time for waiting. Vanstone notes:

> But in John's gospel, at the moment when Jesus is arrested

in the Garden, he is bound there and then . . . [his] unfettered freedom is suddenly changed for bondage, his impalpability to human hands for the literal and physical hold of those hands upon him. At the moment when Jesus is handed over he passes, according to John, from unfettered freedom to total constraint.[12]

In our Faustian culture, which values doing above being, it is illuminating to read either Mark's or John's gospel with Vanstone's eyes. To wait is part of the human condition. But instead of being a regrettable yet inevitable waste, it is a condition for growth, potentially holy and even Christlike. As Vanstone reminds us, 'waiting can be the most intense and poignant of all human experiences – the experience which, above all others, strips us of affectation and self-deception and reveals to us the reality of our needs, our values and ourselves'.[13] As spiritual midwives we will do a great deal of waiting and encourage others to wait, not always in comfort and sometimes in great pain.

One of the great realisations of maturity is the impossibility of autonomy. We work hard to gain and maintain control over our lives. Children assume their parents are magicially omnipotent, and that some day they too will be equally powerful. Adolescents yearn for legal majority on the assumption that the right to drive, drink and vote will bring them freedom from control. Then as adults they discover that freedom remains elusive, attainable perhaps with a better job, a divorce or marriage, children being born or growing up and moving out, a Democrat or a Republican in the White House. Some of us never learn and remain spiritual Micawbers, sure that we are in command and that something will turn up.

But those who are graced with insight glimpse their essential powerlessness, even though outwardly they are achievers, perhaps contributing by their diligence to the common wellbeing. (Teresa of Avila is an outstanding example.) These are the people who often come to us for spiritual direction, baffled by the realisation of the emptiness of their busy lives and frightened by the awareness of their essential impotence. They want to push hard at life, even as they see that this is only making the pain worse and delaying fruition. As spiritual midwives we

---

[12] W. H. Vanstone, *The Stature of Waiting* (London, DLT 1982; and NY, Seabury Press 1983), p. 27.
[13] Ibid. p. 83.

invite them to embrace the passivity of waiting, to breathe lightly and become receptive.

This is not as easy as it sounds, as I realise when I meet Charles, a 'successful' pastor who lives at the edge of burnout. The spiritual and financial vigour of his parish is the envy of his colleagues, his parishioners turn to him with love and respect bordering on veneration, and his bishop thinks of him first when looking for a diocesan committee chairman. Yet Charles finds his life grey and empty. He wonders why he is working so hard, since nothing seems to matter. He wonders why he continues to pray, since that too no longer seems to matter. We both know that he is in a waiting place, but the waiting is hard: Charles is not a man to breathe lightly and stop pushing! Yet his faith is deep, and his trust sufficient. He is willing to hang on. My only task, at this point, is to hang on with him.

Others come who are outwardly as well as spiritually in a waiting place. The frail aged, the physically immobile, and the chronically ill are obvious examples. And the gift of presence is one of our greatest gifts to the dying, whose loved ones and care-givers frequently discourage them from talking about their experiences. The spiritual director can wait and listen, accepting with the dying person the fact of death. We wait too with the bereaved, knowing that grief cannot be hurried but must be lived through. We sit with victims of all kinds, the survivors of violence, abuse and neglect.

Spiritual directors have a ministry of presence to the unemployed whose plight is seen in economic or social terms but often neglected as a spiritual crisis. Similarly, retired persons, although their retirement may be elective and welcomed, find themselves passive, that is, done unto, even in the midst of pleasurable activities. Rather than offering more activities to mask reality, the spiritual director can model acceptance of waiting and invite exploration of its holy emptiness. In less traditional settings, our ministry to the homeless and the imprisoned is also a ministry of patient and attentive waiting.

I realise that that may sound like a prescription for benign neglect of those who – materially or physically – have been given over and find themselves dependent on the actions of others. Nothing could be further from the truth. But spiritual directors are not social workers, physicians or community planners. We cannot and should not try to replace the professionals, programmes and agencies that work to alleviate suffering and promote individual and community wholeness. But we can offer what is inevitably absent from the best-intentioned secular and religious activism: a willingness to wait with others in the face of their powerlessness, 'to sit still, even amid these rocks'.[14]

Transition

The first stage of labour ends in a period of transition, which can be frightening, even terrifying if it is unexpected. Even when it is understood, it is of surprising power. The birthgiver is gripped by tremendous force and feels that she has somehow lost control. Everything is suddenly too big and too powerful. All the weeks of careful preparation and instruction seem inadequate and trivial. The birthgiver had thought she was prepared and 'knew just what to do' – and now it doesn't work! She might even feel betrayed: no one has told her the truth, or perhaps no one has previously confronted and understood the truth. This is a dark, seemingly chaotic period.

In physical birthgiving, transition is the time of greatest discomfort and the time – at least from the birthgiver's viewpoint – of greatest need for the supportive presence of the midwife. In our spiritual lives too, it is a pivotal time. The old ways no longer serve. The comfortable rhythms of worship and solitary prayer feel empty and sterile. Gone is the image of a loving, immanent God, the God who asks: 'Can a woman forget her nursing child, or show no compassion for the child of her womb? Even these may forget, yet I will not forget you. See. I have inscribed you on the palms of my hands. . .'[15]

This vision may have been supplanted by the forbidding image of an angry, punitive God: 'Who can stand before his indignation? Who can endure the heat of his anger? His wrath is poured out like fire, and by him the rocks are broken in pieces.'[16]

Even more likely is the perception of the absence or indifference of God, a God who chooses to distance himself:

Why do you stand so far off, O LORD,
   and hide yourself in time of trouble? . . .
They [the innocent] say in their heart, 'God has forgotten;

[14] T. S. Eliot, 'Ash Wednesday', in *Collected Poems* (London, Faber 1936; NY, Harcourt Brace 1936), p. 121.

[15] Isaiah 49:15–16a.

[16] Nahum 1:6.

he hides his face; he will never notice.'[17]

In all events, what has been learned and diligently practised no longer helps. Nothing is going the way it should, or at least the way we expect it to go. The lonely times of transition can be terrible, for they are times of spiritual homelessness. But they must be lived through, if the birth is to be accomplished.

Neither a midwife nor a spiritual director (yet perhaps a little of both), the poet Rilke offers a moving description of the uncomfortable yet fruitful stage of transition when he speaks of

> moments when something new has entered into us, something unknown; our feelings grow mute in shy perplexity, everything in us withdraws, a stillness comes, and the new, which no one knows, stands in the midst of it and is silent. . . . I believe that almost all our sadnesses are moments of tension that we find paralysing because we no longer hear our surprised feelings living. Because we are alone with the alien thing that has entered our self; because everything intimate and accustomed is for an instant taken away; because we stand in the middle of a transition where we cannot remain standing.[18]

Not surprisingly, transitions are a time when people whose devotion has heretofore been tepid and perfunctory are impelled to seek spiritual direction. Others, if they are well established in a direction relationship, may decide to leave it during a period of transition because they feel that it is somehow 'not working'. Or they may sense that they are poised on the brink of something new, and they are reluctant to take the next step. The woman described in Chapter 2 (p. 57), who stopped direction because it was too costly, was exceptionally self-aware and candid. More commonly, the resistance to change is unconscious and unarticulated. In all cases, however, it is the director's task to discern where the directee is, despite confusing and conflicting signals, and to be aware of both the pain and the promise of transition.

Transitions may be big or small, welcome or unwelcome. Sometimes they can be anticipated, but often they come as a surprise. The obvious ones involve painful loss – death of a loved one, major illness, divorce or other broken relationships,

[17] Psalm 10:1,10.
[18] Rilke, p. 64.

and unemployment. Retirement or other drastic change in manner or place of living are also obvious times of transition. Sometimes the transitions are triggered by positive and welcome changes in the directee's life: the beginning of sobriety, acceptance of one's sexual orientation after a long period of struggle, marriage, the birth of a child, resolution of vocational questions. Instead of the expected smooth sailing, the directee experiences spiritual chaos; everything seems to break down just when he 'has it all together'.

Even when there are no outward triggering events, an apparent loss of faith may signal a time of transition. This is a common experience of seminarians, who find their faith shaken when they expect it to be firmest. It is a painful time, and academic studies do not assuage the pain as the directee is forced to look critically at scripture and history. Similarly, women may find themselves adrift, with all sense of order and meaning taken from them, when they suddenly (or gradually) find themselves cut off by the masculine language of the liturgy. In her essay 'Take Back the Night' Mary E. Giles describes this painful time of liminality:

> In countless situations today women are undergoing the loss of traditional values, systems and relationships to the distress of themselves and their loved ones and to the dismay of those in institutions affected by their experience. When the loss is radical, that is, when it affects our total being, is unplanned and unwanted, reduces us to emotional, intellectual and physical helplessness, leaves us suspended between a darkened past and a dark future so that all of our being rails against the loss, then we are undergoing our dark night. When we cry in anguish 'God, my God,' when we feel empty of all meaning, when we do not know who this God is to whom we dumbly cling, then we are undergoing our dark night. No hint of exotic adventure here, just groping and grasping.[19]

In either case faithful people find themselves in a situation where the old ways no longer serve and from which they cannot retreat. They may be tempted to carry on as if nothing has happened, especially if circumstances encourage conformity. (For example, most seminarians would be wisely reluctant to discuss

---

[19] In *The Feminist Mystic and Other Essays on Women and Spirituality* (NY, Crossroad 1989), pp. 61-2.

their painful and difficult state with the screening bodies who approve them for ordination. In the safety of the spiritual direction relationship, however, they can live through this stage in candour and even come to see its necessity.) But the pain of transition will not go away and must be faced if it is to be got through.

The director can help by naming the transition for what it is: a time of movement from one stage to another, a time of change and transformation. With Rilke, we can counsel that this is a time to be 'still, patient, and open'.[20] Further, even the theologically sophisticated directee can be helped by being reminded that our images of God are indeed images and that, as we see their limitations, we outgrow them. The difficulty comes when we forget that they are images and think we have outgrown God. The spiritually stagnant are able to live in a state of denial, which is tragically also a denial of God and the possibility of growth. But the seeker after God may feel panic: 'Perhaps I have gone too far! I should have been content with the God I had! And even if they were only images, what will replace them?' At its very best this is an unsettling place to be. The ground no longer feels firm beneath one's feet and, as one of my down-to-earth directees says, 'everything is up for grabs'.

As a faithful midwife the director can see patterns and form in seeming formlessness. More important, he knows that the time of transition has a beginning and an end, and that the directee will emerge from it into a new level of clarity. This is a time to share his insights with the directee, who may not believe them but should have sufficient trust to know that these are not words of cheap consolation. Even directees who have not experienced birthgiving are able to understand the imagery of transition as a difficult and confusing stage leading to new life. It remains difficult, but they sense a meaning in its apparent meaninglessness. The midwife-director can help them to let go, to cease to struggle, and to watch attentively for the beginning of the next stage. Transition is a time of surprises; the director can help by pointing out signs in unexpected places.

One of the unwelcome surprises of transition is the loss that inevitably accompanies self-transcendence and new growth. Thus new parents are often surprised by the loss experienced in the birth of a much-wanted child: spontaneity, privacy, self-determination – to name the most obvious. There is even loss

---

[20] Rilke, p. 65.

of identity: to a growing number of people they are now merely somebody's parents.

To accept growth and change in oneself is a kind of departure, a leaving behind of the safe and the known. Sometimes we realise the poignancy of our loss only after the fact, but there is no returning home. One of the treasures in my study is the intact skin of a Virginia black snake, shed as part of the process of growth. (Not all my friends agree on its loveliness.) To grow, indeed to survive, that snake had to leave behind a part of itself. I have no idea whether the shedding hurt or was a relief; but my imagination tells me that it was some of each.

Directees too shed skins and identities if they persevere through the pain of transitions, giving up the safety of outworn images and ways to embrace the new. This is especially poignant since there is often 'nothing wrong' with the old identity or shed skin; it is simply not useful any more and, if clung to, stands in the way of growth and life.

This is an exciting and graced time to be with another as he moves from confusion to clarity, from suspended effort into the active work of the next stage.

The second stage: active work

The second stage begins in the midst of the chaos of transition, with an instinctive awareness of the need to push hard with each contraction. This is the time of active work – as contrasted with the work of waiting. All the birthgiver's attention is concentrated, that is, focussed and centred on the work at hand, which brings with it a sense of excitement, relief and great energy. (However, this might not be apparent to the casual observer, who expects to see signs of pain and exhaustion.)

For the spiritual midwife this is harvest time. The relationship with the directee is well established, with affection and trust on both sides. The long period of waiting is past, and the bleakness of transition has been lived through. The director may feel that his presence is less important, for now, more than ever, the directee is doing the work. This is a good time to remember again what spiritual direction really is: not imposing one's will on another, but respectfully assisting as the path is discerned: which way do I go? What are the signs? Which turn should I take? What is my spiritual direction?

At this stage – and it is important to remember that this is not final, that the whole process will start over again and again

– the direction is clear, the spiritual energy level is high, and the next steps are apparent. For now, the directee has found the rule and discipline that is right for him. For the present moment, at least, he knows who he is. There is a new awareness of his identity in Christ.

This is a time of hard but focused work, as the directee lives into that identity and lives out the insights gained in the earlier stages. It is always clear to me when I work with seminarians that spiritual direction is linked with concern for vocation; for the outer and the inner paths are inextricably tangled. Less obviously but none the less powerfully, all those who seek us out are wrestling with vocation, regardless of their daily occupations. So in a sense, spiritual direction can be seen as vocational guidance – bearing, I hope, little resemblance to the course many of us endured in school.

This stage is not without its own pain. As the inner work progresses the directee experiences ever greater awareness, both of herself but also of all Creation. What may have started as a voyage of self-discovery becomes a journey into the great web of connection. Compassion deepens as the directee grows beyond self-absorption. And compassion is never a cheap or easy gift. What has been seen cannot be unseen; what is known cannot be unknown. Giving birth is not without its dark side: the inevitable changes may be more than the directee has bargained for.

As it is so often, the director's task here is to encourage, quite literally to give heart. In this stage I feel like a coach: you're on the right path, don't stop now, keep going, trust yourself! Don't forget to watch for signs! And don't be surprised at surprises! This is the time when friendship becomes a stronger component in the relationship. It has been there all along, but now the directee knows what the director has known from the beginning: both of us on the same path and doing the same work. The barriers between us are flimsy structures, erected for convenience, or perhaps they are completely illusory. We do not come to this point quickly, but I always find it rewarding. The directee who may have begun our work together with an exaggerated idea of my competence is now willing to see me in my flawed humanity and still love me. After all, he has been doing all the work!

Celebration

Finally the child is born. It is impossible to describe the joy which fills the room at the birth of the child. A midwife friend tells me that the excitement of welcoming new life never grows old. I wept and laughed simultaneously at the first sight of each of my children – beautiful, yet so small, and even to my favourably prejudiced eye slightly comic. All the waiting and work had brought forth this morsel of promise. There is both mystery and absurdity in raw new life, and only those who have not seen it in its newness and rawness can indulge in sentimental and romantic rhapsodies about it. This helpless little creature, dusky purple and rather bizarre, is the fruit of all this waiting, pain, terror and hard work. Surely something more handsome and useful might be expected!

And, of course, the waiting, pain and real work have only begun. Yet the moment of birth is a time for celebration.

We can often make such heavy work of spiritual direction that we neglect the centrality of celebration in it. People find it so easy to say bad things about themselves that it is possible to overlook all the small births, the times for joy and celebration.

Sometimes I wonder what passers-by must think when they see my solemn 'Do Not Disturb' sign on the door and hear laughter coming from within. Surely a spiritual direction meeting is a solemn if not lugubrious occasion for listing faults and uncovering deficiencies. Yet it is self-absorption that leads us to forget the gracious love of God, the giver of new life in the most tired and wounded soul. Even though it is intensely serious (God willing, never lugubrious), spiritual direction will be an occasion for celebration. Eckhart was right when he said, 'Tend only to the birth in you and you will find all goodness and all consolation, all delight, all being and all truth. Reject it and you reject goodness and blessing. What comes to you in this birth brings with it pure being and blessing.'

Not all our directees will be John of the Cross or Teresa of Avila. Most of the people who come to us will be ordinary folk, not candidates for sanctity. Some will bear deep emotional wounds; all will be scarred to some extent. Most of them won't be theologians, and they may be notably lacking in spiritual self-confidence. But as we work together they will bring forth new life – almost always small and helpless and a little bit comic. But at the same time it is mysterious and holy. It is time for rejoicing and celebration, even when the midwife knows that this is just the beginning, the first of many births. Sooner or later, the whole process must begin again.

The mutuality of presence

In her attentive presence, the midwife is not authoritarian, yet she has great authority. She has skill, knowledge and perspective that the birthgiver cannot have, if only because she stands outside the process. She is capable of a loving detachment, but at the same time feels solidarity with the birthgiver. The spiritual midwife, too, needs to experience such solidarity. In her perceptive book on women and spiritual direction, Kathleen Fischer notes that the myth of the expert is more harmful to women than it is to men since women have been conditioned to rely on authority. Hence she urges the de-mystification of the process of spiritual guidance. She cautions especially against patterning the spiritual direction relationship on scientific models with their inevitable emphasis on distance and objectivity, not suitable as prerequisites for healing and personal growth.[21] In other words, even the highly skilled spiritual midwife retains the openness and the emotional involvement of the amateur.

The loving detachment of the spiritual midwife is not synonymous with distance. While the authority of the midwife is a welcome support to the birthgiver, there can be great emotional openness in the solidarity of the non-hierarchical relationship. The spiritual midwife is engaged and emotionally involved, even in her detachment. It cannot be said too often: she is not afraid to be touched.

With the clearer perspective of the midwife who stands outside the process, the spiritual director is able to offer interpretations to the birthgiver. I say 'offer' rather than 'impose', for the director-midwife can never have the **whole** picture. Perhaps the directee is unwilling or unable to disclose some essential part of the story; or perhaps the director's insight is offered prematurely. This is a time for humility and patience on the part of the director, who may fear that a tentative approach lacks strength. Then too both director and directee may be growing uncomfortable with the uncertainty of waiting and may be eager for clarity, even if it is premature and mistaken.

[21] Kathleen Fischer, *Women at the Well: Feminist Perspectives in Spiritual Direction* (NY, Paulist Press 1988), pp. 19–20.

For most of us, loose ends are frightening reminders of our own powerlessness. To name, to label, to classify gives us the illusion of control, even if the closure reached is a false one.

In all events, it is important to leave the directee free to accept or reject our insights. Whether we are right, wrong or premature, it is reassuring to remember that we cannot do too much harm since people rarely hear what they are not ready to hear. At the very least, we have possibly planted a seed. As director-midwives, then, we must be willing to wait for the seed to sprout – if it is supposed to sprout – and grow to maturity, perhaps long after our relationship with the directee has ceased.

While we leave the directee to accept or reject our interpretations, we can help by naming, by simply saying the words. There is truth in the cliché that demons are destroyed or at least rendered powerless by naming them. At the same time we can help liberate the directee from the tyranny of 'shoulds' and 'oughts'. Even if the director is wise enough to avoid prescribing behaviour, the directee may be self-imprisoned. So we hear, 'I shouldn't feel this way, but . . .' or 'I ought not to say this, but . . .' The place of waiting is not necessarily a place of slavish unfreedom nor of repressive denial. The director can gently or briskly clear the air. I find myself saying, 'But you **do** feel this way' or 'Who's going to be offended if you go ahead and say it anyway? God already knows about it, and I probably won't fall off my chair.'

As we wait together in spiritual direction, we are not altogether sure of what we are waiting **for**. Eckhart presents us with the image of a God so filled with love that he is repeatedly born in the empty, welcoming space of the soul. With the sadness and resignation of our own time, philosophy professor Jacob Needleman, author of numerous books dealing with the spiritual search, sounds like a pessimistic Eckhart when he notes that the soul is aborted a thousand times a day.[22] But whether we rejoice with Eckhart in his vision of abundant fecundity or whether we sigh with Needleman at lost promise and wasted life, it is clear that for spiritual directors even seeming emptiness is not sterile. In the times of waiting it is enough if we do nothing more than sit with the birthgiver, offering a literal or spiritual hand to be held.

[22] Jacob Needleman, *Lost Christianity: A Journey of Rediscovery* (San Francisco, Harper & Row 1980), p. 175.

The fear of abandonment

The midwife's comforting hand is welcome, for it is a prevailing fear of labouring women that they will be left alone. More accurately, this is the fear of all of us. With the passing of infancy we learn to control or at least conceal it, but our addictions, physical and spiritual, betray our terror of abandonment. We look to chemicals, food or busyness for solace; or we cling to others in devouring relationships. As I listen to the stories of my directees, it strikes me that we all feel abandoned and that we expend great (and frequently misplaced) spiritual energy trying to deal with our grief and rage at parental desertion. Misplaced, because we do not tap deep enough for the roots of our fear: that we will be abandoned by God.

Thus George is reluctant to explore his relationship with either a loving or neglectful God, insisting that God is not the issue, but rather his cold and abandoning father. His father no doubt **was** cold and abandoning forty-five years ago, but now he is ancient and semi-disabled. While George bears scars and slowly healing wounds – who doesn't? – he is a man of considerable gifts. He resists my suggestion that he seeks psychotherapy to gain insight into his relationship with his father, who serves a useful purpose: as a screen and diversion to keep George from facing his deeper fear. The God he has created and keeps on a shelf is beneficent, albeit rather ineffectual, and not nearly so powerful – or so absorbing – as Daddy. Perhaps some day he will feel strong enough to put his father aside, if not to forgive him, and look squarely at his relationship with a God of love and terror. Perhaps with the Psalmist he will then be able to pray: 'How long, O Lord? will you forget me for ever? how long will you hide your face from me? How long shall I have perplexity in my mind, and grief in my heart, day after day?'[23] A great barrier will then be broken, and a frozen place in George will begin to melt. I am not sure, however, that this can happen unless he is willing to seek professional help to heal the hurts he carries within him. At present he is not ready to give them up.

Not all directees present themselves in George's stark terms, but many share his reluctance to articulate their sense of abandonment by God. Here, as elsewhere, they are quick to blame themselves and suppress any feelings of anger. If they feel cut off, they must have done something to deserve it. The director

[23] Psalm 13:1–2.

can help here by reminding them that their experience is not
unique, not in a way that seeks to minimise their pain but rather
to diminish their isolation. The Psalmist is a splendid help here.
So many of us get stuck at the familiar 23rd, usually words of
great comfort, but bitter irony to the person who feels that the
Lord is **not** his shepherd and that all those good things prom-
ised in the Psalm are not coming to him – at least not now! We
can offer relief to those suffering from a sense of abandonment
when we remind them of the 22nd Psalm:

My God, my God, why have you forsaken me?
    and are so far from my cry
    and from the words of my distress?
O my God, I cry in the daytime, but you do not answer,
    by night as well, but I find no rest.

Although the psalm begins in anguished despair, it moves to a
firm but not sentimental place of strength: 'My soul shall live
for him.' For those who find even this a travesty of false cheer-
fulness, there is Psalm 88, ending on its note of darkness: 'My
friend and my neighbour you have put away from me, and darkness is my only companion.'

I hasten to note – yet again – that the spiritual director is
neither a physician nor a psychotherapist. The spiritual,
emotional and physical can be wonderfully intermingled; and
a sense of abandonment by God can go hand in hand with a
clinical depression. We owe it to our directees to see them as
whole people and not to conspire with them in spiritualising
what is not spiritual. So I find it quite appropriate to enquire
about both general and emotional health and to make referrals.
A wise psychiatrist friend once told me to be especially attentive
when I felt myself bored or fatigued in a conversation. Of
course, I might **be** tired or possibly the directee **is** boring; but
quite likely I am seeing someone who is clinically depressed.
It's been a good rule of thumb.

(It helps to have resources if I am going to make referrals; the
Yellow Pages are not good enough. As a minimum, the director
needs to have confidence in at least two internists, male and
female; at least one psychiatrist; and several psychotherapists
– gay people, survivors of sexual abuse, families, single people,
those recovering from addiction, all have their special needs
and vulnerabilities.)

Perhaps most important, the director can in a modest way

model God's faithfulness, even when the directee feels that God is absent. We do this best by our attentiveness, which shows that we value the person, take him seriously, and hear his story critically but without judging. If we are careful to maintain a loving distance, we do not fall into the trap of promising more than we can give or of becoming inappropriately enmeshed in the directee's life. For the person who feels abandoned, by God and by others, our faithful attentiveness is enough.

Present at the thresholds

Now and then someone asks me how I ended up doing what I am doing. When I reflect on this question I am always amazed at the great economy of the spirit. Even as there is the law of the conservation of matter, so there is a similar conservation of the spirit: nothing gets lost, nothing gets wasted; seeming loss is really transformation. At one time I was sure that my ministry lay with the dying. I had considerable experience with the frail aged and was comfortable with them. I discovered that the sights, sounds and smells of suffering in a large urban hospital did not repel me. After many vigils in the Intensive Care Unit as the line on the monitor flattened out, I learned that I was not frightened to be present at that threshold.

From my own experience I knew about the other threshold, but only gradually did I become aware, like Eliot, of their bond:

. . . were we led all that way for
Birth or Death? There was a Birth, certainly,
We had evidence and no doubt. I had seen birth and death,
But had thought they were different. . .[24]

To be sure, birth and death imagery are linked in the gospels and in Paul's letters. But it was with some surprise that I realised that, as a spiritual director, I was helping people to be born, give birth – and to die. The classical language of spirituality speaks of 'unselfing', that is, shedding the outgrown skins and discarding whatever clutters us and weights us down. It is a kind of death, repeated again and again if we remain spiritually alive. The spiritual director can be a gentle assistant.

Then too, we are literally helping people to prepare to die. This is obvious when I spend time with my dear friend Ellen

[24] T. S. Eliot, 'The Gift of the Magi', in *Collected Poems*, p. 126.

(whom I have mentioned earlier). In her extreme age and bodily frailty she is permitting me to accompany her to a place where I could not otherwise go; at least, not yet. I am not sure, in this case, which of us is the midwife. It is less obvious in work with the young and healthy, who might squirm or laugh uneasily at the idea of spiritual direction as 'preparation for a good death'. Yet each small threshold crossed is a taste of death. Each inevitable experience of loss is a foreshadowing. In great ways and small, we come as close as we can to practising our crossing of the great second threshold.

So, when I am asked how I got to my present spot, I respond, 'I felt called to work with the dying.' And let it go at that.

A final word

Throughout history it has been a paradox that the midwife is both important and insignificant. Shiphrah and Puah, sought out by Pharaoh, literally held the future in their hands. By the late Middle Ages the Dominican inquisitors were so frightened of these older women who were present at the threshold of new life that they were singled out for special condemnation. Thus the writers of the *Malleus Maleficarum*, the infamous fifteenth-century handbook for the detection of witches, caution that 'no one does more harm to the Catholic Faith than midwives. For when they do not kill children, then, as if for some other purpose, they take them out of the room and, raising them up in the air, offer them to devils.'[25] Later they speak of midwives, who 'surpass all other witches in their crimes. . . And the number of them is so great that, as has been found from their confessions, it is thought that there is scarcely any tiny hamlet in which at least one is not to be found.'[26]

Clearly the midwife had a kind of power that was simultaneously frightening to the repressive authorities and comforting to a labouring woman. Yet midwives have never been grand or impressive figures. They have not sought the power which is theirs. They are humble.

Similarly the spiritual midwife is humble and, like her

---

[25] Quoted in Kors and Peters, *Witchcraft in Europe 1100–1700: A Documentary History* (University of Pennsylvania Press 1972), p. 127.
[26] Ibid. p. 184.

practical sister, always clear about her own identity and role in the drama of birthing. For spiritual directors the Holy Spirit is the true director.

4

WOMEN AND SPIRITUAL DIRECTION

So God created humankind in his image; in the image of God created he them; male and female created he them. (Genesis 1:27)

Woman, do you not know that you are Eve? You are the devil's gateway. How easily you destroyed man, the image of God! (Tertullian)

For as many of you as were baptised into Christ have put on Christ. There is neither Jew nor Greek, there is neither slave nor free, there is neither male nor female; for you are all one in Christ Jesus. (Galatians 3:27–28)

She who does not believe is a woman and should be designated by the name of her sex, whereas she who believes progresses to perfect manhood, to the measure of adulthood in Christ. (Ambrose of Milan)

Let a woman learn in silence with all submissiveness. I permit no woman to teach or to have authority over men; she is to keep silent. For Adam was formed first, then Eve; and Adam was not deceived, but the woman was deceived and became a transgressor. Yet woman will be saved through bearing children, if she continues in faith and love and holiness, with modesty. (1 Timothy 2:11–15)

. . . he appeared first to Mary Magdalene, from whom he had cast out seven demons. She went out and told those who had been with him, as they mourned and wept. But when they heard that he was alive and had been seen by her, they would not believe it. (Mark 16:9–11)

IN MY PREVIOUS INCARNATION as a college professor I was proud of my ability to speak and write the language of the dominant group in our society. While secretly I thought and read and wrote from the perspective of my own inner experience, professionally I suppressed any signs of dangerous otherness. I recall – now with some chagrin – an intended compliment from one of my professors in graduate school: 'Miss Beltz, you think like a man.' In those days, if women were in any way different, the less said about it the better; and those who wished to participate in any field beyond the narrowly domestic worked hard to conform. Times are changing. All of us, men and women, are seeing with new eyes.

I know that my way of doing spiritual direction is affected if not determined by my being a woman, a woman with my particular mix of life experience. Further, it must be clear to any reader of these pages that most of the people who seek me out are women. I have made no statistical studies, but I suspect that more women than men seek spiritual direction, regardless of the sex of the director. Certainly most of our enquiries and requests for referrals at the Center for Christian Spirituality come from women. Increasingly women (and particularly lay women) are exploring their vocations in our training programmes.

Although there is growing awareness that women's spirituality is distinctive, it has been until very recently largely unexplored. As I have already noted, the best-known works on spiritual formation and direction have been written by men. But women's voices have begun to be heard in the past few years. Perhaps the seminal work in the investigation of women's spirituality was written by an academic psychologist rather than a theologian and intended for a lay readership: Carol Gilligan's *In a Different Voice* (1982) offered a fresh vision of women as moral decision-makers. For me and many of my friends, this was an 'aha!' book: we saw ourselves in it, and behold, it was very good. Mary Field Belenky and her collaborators have given us a valuable study in *Women's Ways of Knowing* (1986), doing for epistemology what Gilligan had done for ethics: not only do we judge differently, we **learn** differently. And that's all right, too! Madonna Kolbenschlag's writings are classified as 'Psychology/Women's Studies' by her publisher, but *Kiss Sleeping Beauty Goodbye* (1978) is a primer in women's spirituality.

The dam has been broken, or at least cracked; and works by women about women's spirituality proliferate. But there is a lot of catching up to be done, and the valuable work of such writers as Joann Wolski Conn, Kathleen Fischer and Sandra Schneiders are just the beginning. From working with many male colleagues and reading their books, I am convinced that women function differently as directors – not better, not worse, but differently. We bring our special gifts, our unique perspective, and our vulnerabilities. And from spending thousands of hours with women as directees, I am equally convinced that they bring special gifts, perspectives and vulnerabilities.

It would be a great loss if increased consciousness of the distinct qualities of women's spirituality led to some kind of rigid separatism. As men and women, we are completed by each other; this is as true in the spiritual direction relationship as in all others. There are times when women work most fruitfully and honestly with other women, and there are times when the challenge of otherness in the director is beneficial. Above all, we need to know each other's stories. Most women know the stories and language of men. Just as I learned in graduate school to function well in a context and terminology that was not my own, most women know the accepted language of religious observance and traditional spirituality. Yet we cannot expect openness and sensitivity from men until they are equally acquainted with women's spirituality and their language for it. Some male directors may persist in the (often unconsciously) arrogant assumption that their language, perceptions and experience are the norm; women who turn to them for spiritual direction will be patronised or dismissed outright. Fortunately, however, a growing number of men are becoming aware of the differences – the differences of language, life experience and experience of God, ways of praying and ways of sinning. Their eagerness to know and to understand is a great step towards wholeness and reconciliation in the Church.

In this chapter I will reflect first about women as spiritual directors: how their way of working differs from that of their male colleagues, what their special gifts might be, and what their limitations. Then, and more extensively, I will write from my experience of women as directees.

Women as spiritual directors: the listeners

Women are listeners! As a member of the seminary admissions committee, I interview many prospective students (who are usually also prospective clergy). I am also asked frequently to meet people in the very early stages of exploration of their possible vocation. Again and again I am struck by the number of women – of all ages, levels of education and professional experience – who are drawn to some kind of listening ministry. They can easily envision themselves as chaplains in hospitals, hospices, schools and prisons. They may need supervision to help understand their own motives; but, upon admission to the seminary, these same women perform superbly in the practical and pastoral parts of their training. However impatient they may become with systematic theology or clumsy with scriptural exegesis, their gifts as listeners are beyond question.

These gifts are deeply inbred, and they carry with them the potential for misuse. Traditionally, girl-children have been socialised to 'be there for others', which includes attentiveness to their words. At least at certain stages in a woman's developing self-awareness, this careful listening is a valid way to learn about herself. So the relationship is less altruistic than it might appear: in addition to the satisfaction of being 'generous' and 'good' (questionable motives for the mature spiritual director) the woman is achieving something important to her own development. The authors of *Women's Ways of Knowing* observe:

> Women typically approach adulthood with the understanding that the care and empowerment of others is central to their life's work. Through listening and responding, they draw out the voices and minds of those they help to raise up. In the process, they often come to hear, value and strengthen their own voices and minds as well.[1]

This feels very safe, for the woman need reveal little of herself as she listens. Since she is primarily interested in taking in and absorbing from the speaker, she appears and indeed is non-judgmental. In consequence, others are drawn to her and trust her.

I am convinced that many women feel the call to a listening ministry, be it a chaplaincy or spiritual direction, when they find others turning to them and trusting them as sympathetic listeners. Even when unconscious needs are being met, the call to ministry is often a valid one. The impetus is troubling only if it remains unexamined. At this point, the sought-after listener is by no means a spiritual director; and if she thinks she is, she risks pretentiousness and self-deception. But her gifts of listening as an unconscious means of self-understanding can be a

---

[1] Mary Field Belenky *et al.*, *Women's Ways of Knowing* (NY, Basic Books 1986), p. 48.

fruitful first step towards ministry, as she grows to a sufficiently secure sense of self to be able to put that self aside. She no longer needs to **use** others to learn about herself, although increasing self-knowledge is an inevitable concomitant of doing spiritual direction. Rather, she can employ her highly developed listening skills in a spirit of loving detachment. She can listen **maternally**.

I am indebted to the authors of *Women's Ways of Knowing* for the concept of maternal listening and, more broadly, maternal conversation. Their studies indicate that women tend to talk about personal matters with their mothers and impersonal matters with their fathers. When they do happen to discuss personal topics with their fathers, the latter tell their daughters what they ought to do:

> That such differences between mothers and fathers are so common may be accounted for by the fact that many men are used to being the expert, while many women are used to consulting others; many men are interested in how experience is generalised and universalised, while many women are interested in what can be learned from the particular; and the work of men frequently involves maintaining or increasing the status differential between persons, while the life work of many women focuses on maternal practice, where the main goal is to bring the smallest, least members up into relations of equality.[2]

The authors emphasise that this is not a sign of greater caring on the part of the mothers or coldness in the fathers. Rather, the mothers try to help on the daughters' terms, while the fathers' help is offered on the fathers' terms.

Maternal conversation is an appropriate mode for spiritual direction. The director is willing to listen, that is, to be present to the directee where he is. By the very nature of the relationship, the director has been given tacit permission to ask questions. (This is in contrast to conventionally polite conversation, which forbids asking anything that really matters.) But they must be the right questions, asked in a spirit of attentive love. In her essay on 'Forms of the Implicit Love of God', Simone Weil writes compellingly of this generous and compassionate attentiveness as manifested in the story of the Good Samaritan:

[2] Ibid. p. 184.

> Christ taught us that the supernatural love of our neigh-
> bour is the exchange of compassion and gratitude which
> happens in a flash between two beings, one possessing and
> the other deprived of human personality. One of the two
> is only a little piece of flesh, naked, inert, and bleeding
> beside a ditch; he is nameless, no one knows anything
> about him. Those who pass by scarcely notice it. . . Only
> one stops and turns his attention towards it. The actions
> that follow are just the automatic effect of this moment of
> attention. The attention is creative.[3]

While the people who come to us for spiritual direction are
rarely in such dire straits as the injured man in the parable, by
our own attentive love we can help them towards wholeness. As
the authors of *Women's Ways of Knowing* observe, 'It is through
attentive love, the ability to ask, "What are you going
through?" and the ability to hear the answer that the reality of
the child [read: directee] is both created and respected.'[4] The
questions are not a means of amassing data, but rather are
open-ended and compassionate, an invitation to trust. The
director must be willing to hear the answer and resist the temptation to offer glib advice.

Even the experienced director should not lose sight of the
perils that accompany her (and also his) gifts as a listener. It is
gratifying to be trusted and heady to be relied upon. Human
life and lives are infinitely fascinating; and, unless the director
works out of her own satisfying context of relationships, there
is the danger of becoming a spiritual voyeur, using and
feeding upon the other. So she listens intently to the directee's
story, never bored, but always disinterested. My inner alarm
bells sound when I find myself growing curious, taking
sides or becoming emotionally invested. I know that I am
about to step over an invisible line and that the delicate
balance can be destroyed. Even if my words and actions remain
correct, I am in danger of **using** the directee for my own grati-
fication.

[3] Simone Weil, *Waiting for God* (London, 1951; NY, Harper Colophon 1973),
pp. 146–7.
[4] Belenky *et al.* p. 189.

Women as spiritual directors: the outsiders

Over the centuries women have kept the Church going by their faithfulness, but have lived their inner lives around its edges. (One of my less reverent fantasies about the Last Supper includes some women in the kitchen, their faces rosy with the heat of the oven, peeping through the pass-through to watch and eavesdrop, perhaps to be awarded with a word of praise and spatter of applause for the excellent roast lamb.) They are included, yet there is always a 'Yes, but . . .' The old myth of uncleanness is now in poor taste, but it lingers on in woman's otherness which – up to now – the Church has not been able to incorporate.

Not surprisingly, the idea that women might be spiritual guides gains slow acceptance.[5] Yet is is frequently their very otherness that makes them able and open as spiritual directors, especially effective in ministry on the margins and in the interstices. Their own experience makes them work well with those who are disaffected, who do not trust the institutional Church, even though they may be drawn to it. Most particularly, they are accessible to other women, both the gently despairing and the victims of abuse. When the directee is burdened by shame, she may feel safest with another woman, particularly a lay woman. And the director will hear again and again, 'I just couldn't talk to Father about this. It's embarrassing, and I know it's not very spiritual, but . . .'

Sandra Schneiders has written perceptively about the special quality of women's ministry, resulting from their centuries-long exclusion from the inner circles. Having never been 'ritualised' their ministry is often unrecognised and unnamed, but nevertheless powerful because it is of necessity personalised. She observes that 'it belongs to the very nature of ritual that it largely subsumes the individuality of the ritualist. Women's ministry has never been anything other than the personal service of one human being to another in the name of Christ.'[6] His ministry provides the model for the director who is 'other' and most at home at the margins and in the crevices. It too was non-ritualised and 'characterised by a gentleness and a power-

---

[5] Tilden Edwards' observations have already been noted. See *Spiritual Friend*, p. 206.
[6] Sandra M. Schneiders, 'Effects of Women's Experience on Spirituality', in *Women's Spirituality*, p. 34.

lessness that were singularly revelatory of the true God'.[7] Schneiders goes on to point out that

> the non-ritualised ministry of women has contributed very little to the pervasive image of the Christian God as a stern, even violent, father-figure bent on exact justice and retribution. Indeed, experienced spiritual directors know that, when a person's violent God-image begins to be healed, that healing is often effected by, and expressed in, a recognition in God of the qualities one has experienced in the women in one's life – mother, sister, wife or lover.[8]

There is freedom for a woman director in her marginality and powerlessness. She can be open to all sorts and conditions of men and women, feeling no need to condemn or exclude because some official standard is not met. This makes her open and sensitive to the stories and experience of those society has pushed to the edges or tried to render invisible – the frail aged, the abused, gay men and lesbians.

What will happen as more women's voices are heard, as women move from the edges towards the centre, as they become equal partners in the establishment? Will the Church change and grow towards wholeness because of their true inclusion, or will women lose their spiritual freedom as they lose their marginality? In the meantime, women still work to be taken seriously. This is especially true for lay women whose gifts in spiritual direction are often unrecognised or undervalued. It is easier for directors who are ordained or are members of a religious order; a clerical collar or a religious habit makes a statement of authority. While academic courses or an impressive certificate cannot form a director when the innate gift is not there, I rejoice that there are avenues to some kind of certification for lay persons (usually women). The authority is already there; but seminary study, programmes such as those at the Center for Christian Spirituality or Shalem Institute, or a unit of Clinical Pastoral Education can set a woman director free to acknowledge and claim it. This is not to minimise the importance of formal study or of work done under supervision. However, the chief value of training in spiritual direction is to legitimise this ministry in a time obsessed with credentials. The

---

[7] Ibid. p. 35.
[8] Ibid. pp. 34–5.

desert abbas and ammas knew who they were, and so did everybody else.

Women as spiritual directors: the mothers

While Jesus is our primary model for the spiritual director as
teacher, there are others, even those and perhaps especially
those who guided him. It is easy to overlook his first teacher:
his mother. Like all infants, he learned about being human from
looking into her face, hearing her voice, feeling her touch. She
was the first person to teach him about steadfast love. From
her, he learned about feeding, washing and healing – surely
women's work, yet an essential part of his ministry. Even as the
scholars in the temple taught the twelve-year-old of the
abstract, unknowable God, so his mother provided ground-
edness in physical, human experience.

This awareness helps me in doing spiritual direction. It
keeps before me the unquestioning and tenacious love of
mothers.

Yet even with the example of Mary, along with the desert
ammas and Julian of Norwich, before me I approach the idea of
spiritual director as mother with trepidation. Parental imagery
carries so much baggage, largely negative. Surely spiritual
directors are not expected to infantilise those who turn to them.
Or to smother them with affection. But such behaviour is not
good mothering. Good mothering enables the child to develop
his capabilities, grow to maturity, and move away from
reliance on the mother. My Virginia neighbours, the black
bears, are competent mothers: the cubs are nurtured as long
as necessary and then sent briskly on their way. The mother
bears may be lacking in tenderness, but they understand their
role!

While I haven't reached the state of detachment of the black
bear, I have spent too long with the day-to-day realities of
mothering to be sentimental about it. If I am now perceived as
a motherly person I would prefer to be seen as a desert amma.
Most important, for good or ill, I know that my own experience
in mothering colours the way in which I do spiritual direction.
(If I seem to be excluding a large segment of the population,
Eckhart reminds us that we can all be mothers. While the
experience of bearing and nurturing a child is unique,
maternal ways of being are available to all of us, men and
women.)

Being a mother calls for patience. The whole process begins with a long wait! Then, even after the child is born, he develops slowly. Simply holding up his head is a major achievement, and it is hard for the mother to realise that this small creature will one day become mobile, acquire speech and even understand computers. Each small step towards maturity and self-sufficiency is cause for rejoicing. The wise mother knows the stages of development and never expects the impossible.

So she is able to put her own needs aside and meet the child where he is. In biological motherhood this is easier said than done: most of us fail several times a day. The maternal spiritual director has a better chance of consistency and success, if only because the parameters of her work are clearly defined, and she can be sure of some respite. Biological motherhood is total.

Some of my learnings from motherhood transfer smoothly to the ministry of spiritual direction. Almost automatically I found myself practising what the authors of *Women's Ways of Knowing* call maternal conversation. Sometimes it's hard to ask the right questions, but I have learned that the wrong ones can kill love and spontaneity. I have learned too that small people feel abandonment, no matter how much they are cherished; and they can easily persuade themselves that they are unworthy of love. I have learned that gentleness can accomplish a lot more than harshness.

Sometimes I wonder if I am sufficiently directive as a spiritual director. Confrontation is fashionable these days, yet it simply doesn't fit the maternal style. As I have already noted, people come looking for a really tough director, going to great lengths to explain their spiritual untrustworthiness and consequent need to be kept in line. I warn them that I am quite capable of confronting them now and then, but not to count on it. Some wisely decide that I am not the right person for them. Others stay with me and discover that they can do a pretty good job of keeping themselves in line.

Mothers provide safety and reassurance, even when their confidence is unwarranted by external circumstances. The lay theologian Margaret Hebblethwaite instinctively greeted her firstborn, seconds after his birth, with the words, 'Dominic Paul, it's all right, it's all right.' Upon reflection she observed that this 'common message of comfort from a mother to her

child' is a metaphysical statement.[9] It's all right – words probably spoken by mothers as Herod's soldiers searched the houses
of Bethlehem for baby boys, by mothers in cattle trucks *en route*
to death camps, by mothers in all times and all places kissing
small hurts to make them well. Not surprisingly, at least one
translation of a crucial passage from Julian of Norwich
makes the same metaphysical statement and provides it with
context:

> On one occasion the good Lord said, 'Everything is going
> to be all right.' On another, 'You will see for yourself that
> every sort of thing will be all right.' In these two sayings
> the soul discerns various meanings.
>
> One is that he wants us to know that not only does he
> care for great and noble things, but equally for little and
> small, lowly and simple things as well. This is his meaning:
> '*Everything* will be all right.' We are to know that the least
> things will not be forgotten.[10]

In their instinctively murmured words of comfort, mothers
do not deny the pain, uncertainty, even the terror of life. They
simply remind the child – and themselves – that at the deepest
level it truly is all right. We can do this as spiritual directors,
not in false cheeriness or denial, but by our own steadfastness.
If **we** believe with Julian that, in spite of everything, it will be
all right, we need not say the words. We can embody them.
Finally a great learning from motherhood is the realisation that
we have our children only on loan, that they are not really 'our'
children. It's good to remember that we have directees in the
same kind of sacred trust.

Women as directees

I have already noted that the preponderance of those seeking
referral to a spiritual director are women. If male clergy and
seminarians (a special population required or at least strongly
encouraged to have a director) are excluded, the disproportion
is even more striking. These are almost always women for
whom the old ways no longer serve. A generation ago they
might have been immersed in traditional 'women's work' in the

[9] Margaret Hebblethwaite, *Motherhood and God* (London, Geoffrey Chapman
1984), pp. 31–3.
[10] Julian of Norwich, *Revelations of Divine Love*, tr. Clifton Wolters (Penguin
1966), p. 109.

parish. They would not have expected to hear their experience addressed in sermons or comprehended in the liturgy. Now they are looking for something more. This may manifest itself in a sense of call to the ordained ministry, which is possibly a mature and valid one. Often, however, they are dealing seriously for the first time with a deeper call to ministry *per se*, which may manifest itself mistakenly as the call to ordination. The institutional Church has not been helpful to these women; for, while lip-service is paid to the importance and legitimacy of lay ministry, the powerful unspoken message remains one of clericalism: the **real** minister is the one up front on Sunday morning. The power and urgency of the call are unmistakable, and the woman knows that she must **do** something about it. Left on her own, she can see few paths other than ordination. The spiritual director can assist her in the work of discernment by helping her to a broader vision of ministry.

It is easy to be dismissive of the stereotype 'mid-life crisis', forgetting the extraordinary promise of this crucial time. Regardless of the nature of their call, these women are to be heard and taken seriously, for they are wrestling with issues of vocation. God is calling them to something. What? Something more than turning up faithfully on Sunday morning, and something more than devoted committee work. But what? They are impelled to move beyond the safety of either traditional parish roles or bland indifference to risk embarking on a search for intimacy with God which may only increase their present loneliness.

For I am struck by the isolation of these women. Many are without a life partner, rarely by choice. To some extent, they turn to God in their very human loneliness, but it would be cruelly reductionist to minimise their yearning on this account. Further, I am touched by the spiritual isolation of many married women who seem to 'have everything' – a relatively stable marriage, material possessions in abundance, and standing in their secular community. They enter spiritual direction not so much out of greedy desire to add God to their already considerable possessions, but from a sense of emptiness. They too deserve to be taken seriously.

It is easy to dismiss women who are obviously needy and often inarticulate. Some directors see their yearning for God as pathological and want to pass them on quickly to psychotherapists or marriage counsellors. But there is a distinctive quality to a woman's spiritual search which merits attention. Madonna

Kolbenschlag observes that women seek advice and counsel much more frequently than men and that they turn to an exploration of their spirituality, indeed to religion in general, as personally therapeutic. It is possible, then, for them to get stuck in what she calls a 'passive-receptive mode'.[11]

While there is much wisdom in Kolbenschlag's observations, I would argue that women must be the recipients of healing before or at least concurrently with becoming its dispensers. While their need for approval initially may be excessive, they can and must grow into the assurance that they are worthy, known and accepted before they can move on to the next step. The director, male or female, lay or ordained, must not let them get stuck in the passive-receptive mode.

When women come seeking spiritual direction I sense in them a great yearning, regardless of their relative woundedness or health, their zeal or their passivity. They are yearning to be known, to be able to say with Jeremiah, 'Yet you, O Lord, are in the midst of us, and we are called by your name.'[12] They are yearning to know that their voice will be heard. But their experience in the Church over the centuries has created a painful impediment. As I noted in my discussion of women's special qualities as directors, the voices of authority have been traditionally male: preachers, pastors, theologians, confessors, and spiritual directors. As Martin Smith comments in *Reconciliation*:

> The historical monopoly men have had of the official teaching roles in the church, a monopoly now happily on the way to being broken, has meant, among other things, that women have usually been required to understand their relationship with God and their ethical and spiritual

---

[11] *Kiss Sleeping Beauty Good-Bye*, p. 181 *et passim*. She develops the concept further: 'Because they do not see themselves as agents of spiritual energy – as divinised, transcending centres – religious experience becomes something to be applied to oneself, or which one applies to life's hurts like a poultice. Women see themselves as the chief recipients rather than as dispensers of the healing, celebrating and teaching medicines of organised religion. . . Their need for approval and security generates a doctor-patient relation between clerics and women. . . This hierarchical, therapeutic relationship epitomises the patriarchal closure of women, their fixation as the primary votives of sacred dispensation and spiritual direction. If women are to mature in the spiritual life, this unauthentic, non-autonomous pattern of relationship must be broken' (p. 182).

[12] Jeremiah 14:9.

responses in terms that do not fit the special dynamics of women's lives.[13]

The exclusion of women has sometimes been the result of benign neglect; more often, however, it reflects contempt, fear and cruelty – and complete disregard of the message of the gospel.

The chilling words of Ambrose of Milan at the beginning of this chapter make it clear that there was no such thing as a spiritually mature woman (see p. 113). Ambrose sounds like a fourth-century brother of the professor who admired my 'thinking like a man' – until we remember that the most commonly cited studies of faith development and ethical decision-making (Erikson, Fowler, Kohlberg) purport to speak for all, but are based on studies of male experience. On the commonly used scales, most women remain 'immature' in their faith development.[14]

By and large, too, traditional acculturation inhibits growth towards true maturity, and women are discouraged from becoming fully themselves. To be sure, this occurs with ever greater subtlety as legal barriers are removed. According to Irenaeus, 'The glory of God is a human being fully alive.' But women do not easily find the opportunity to be alive in this way. The glorification of the child-woman pervades our culture. With the help of the cosmetics and fitness industries, the mature woman must work hard not to show her life experience in her face or her body.

An even more insidious barrier to maturity is the ideal of living for others. As Joann Wolski Conn observes:

[13] Martin Smith, *Reconciliation* (Mowbray 1986; US, Cowley 1985), p. 77. In a similar vein J. Neville Ward observes: 'All Christian dogmatic theology has been written by men. Women such as St Teresa of Avila and Mother Julian of Norwich have had an important place in the realm of mystical theology, and they have figured repeatedly in the drama of Christian martyrdom; but it cannot be denied that theology, ecclesiology and the main tradition of Christian spirituality are the creation of men. There have been historical and cultural reasons for this masculine dominance in the past, but they are rapidly ceasing to be cogent, and a new situation emerges in which women can redress this imbalance in theology and spirituality', *The Following Plough* (Epworth 1978; US, Cowley 1984), p. 94.

[14] According to James Fowler's study, the highest stage of ethical decision-making is based on adherence to an abstract principle. Carol Gilligan has demonstrated that mature women are conscious of relationship and connections, rather than abstractions, in their formation of judgments.

Christian teaching and practice, instead of promoting women's maturity, has significantly contributed to its restriction. Women have consistently been taught to value only one type of religious development – self-denial and sacrifice of one's own needs for the sake of others. Whereas men have been taught to couple self-denial with prophetic courage to resist undue authority, women have been taught to see all male authority as God-given and to judge that assertion of their own desires was a sign of selfishness and pride.[15]

For centuries this has been instilled in girl-children as the meaning and purpose of life. I know women who accept a life of utter self-effacement without questioning the purpose or the object of the sacrifice. Mildred is such a woman: everything in her life is devoted to her husband. She does not like to be reminded that she is thereby confusing him with God and that the name of the sin is idolatry.

Finally, while there are scriptural grounds in support of self-sacrifice, **there must first be a mature self to sacrifice**. The spiritual director can assist in the development of that self.

Some issues of language

Traditionally, then, women are not socialised to value themselves, their insights, their opinions, their questions. Writing about the diffidence and self-deprecation of women in a typical academic setting, historian Gerda Lerner notes that in their muteness they are saying: 'I do not deserve to take up time and space.'[16]

Women bring this bearing to spiritual direction as well as to the classroom. The directee often comes with a sense of unworthiness, of not measuring up – to what, she is not sure. She may think in terms of an abstract, judging, patriarchal God and thereby face a split between who and where she really is in terms of life experience and deep concerns and who and where she thinks she SHOULD be. This is especially poignant in

---

[15] Conn, ed., *Women's Spirituality: Resources for Christian Development* (NY, Paulist 1986), p. 4.

[16] Gerda Lerner, *The Majority Finds Its Past*, pp. 243–4. Similarly Carol Gilligan notes that women are unwilling to make moral judgments, feeling they have no right to do so. Thus they exclude themselves from decision-making (*In a Different Voice*, p. 16 *et passim*).

matters of love and charity, where the directee finds herself taking a softer line than the perceived 'right' one. Thus Marilyn came to me wrestling with her conscience: she felt guilty that she was unable to judge gay people harshly, even though her strict religious upbringing had taught her that they merited condemnation. Simply articulating her dilemma, in the safety of our time together, enabled her to stand on her own spiritual feet. This was her first joyous step towards the liberating vision of a God who hates nothing he has made.

The directee may present herself as tentative and indirect, almost to the point of playing guessing games. The director may be tempted to dismiss her as 'not serious' or immature, particularly if he is unaware or contemptuous of the characteristics of women's language.[17] I have already noted the bilingualism achieved by women who wish to be taken seriously: they become fluent in the language of the dominant group and suppress as inappropriate their natural speech, at least in 'important' conversations. More pervasive and usually unconscious is a verbal tentativeness, an unwillingness to take responsibility for what is said. This is achieved by the frequent use of 'rather', 'perhaps' or 'some'. Statements of conviction lose their strength when introduced with 'I think' instead of 'I know'. There is also the attempt to involve the listener in statements and to secure his agreement; this is done by ending the sentence interrogatively, either in actual words (Isn't it?) or by a rising inflection of voice.[18] Jane was a directee capable of making strong statements and asking powerful questions and then demolishing them before any response was possible. Her entrapment in 'woman's language' made her appear shallow and indecisive, a spiritual dilettante. Even when I understood the situation and felt great liking for her, I found myself fighting irritation at the teasing hesitancy of her speech. Our work together progressed only when I pointed out what I was observing and asked permission to draw her attention to it each time she slipped. She had been unaware of her tendency to verbal self-destruction and gratefully agreed to my plan.

The director can and must help by holding a woman responsible for her statements; this means, first, assuring her that it is

[17] In addition to my own observations, I am greatly indebted to Robin Lakoff's small but seminal book, *Language and Woman's Place* (NY, Harper Torchbooks 1975).

[18] Lakoff observes that this intonational pattern is found in English only among women speakers (ibid. p. 17).

safe to be responsible. I am convinced that much of women's tentative speech arises from fear of her own anger, that somehow there will be terrible retribution – divine or otherwise – if she reveals herself as a strong person. Occasionally I remind Susanne, who is expert at indirect and hesitant speech, that God already knows her dangerous thoughts and has so far resisted zapping her, and that she has nothing to fear from me. I will be delighted when we have grown sufficiently in love and trust for Susanne to feel safe to rage at God or at me. It's coming, but it's still a long way off.

We need to listen for questions as well, perhaps mostly for the unasked questions. Women have had little to do with positing the questions or designing the agendas of theology. (A case in point: if Priscilla or Thecla had written our epistles instead of Paul, I suspect there would have been a very incarnational treatment of the incarnation and relatively little about circumcision, of the heart or elsewhere.) Consequently they have answers for questions that are never asked and questions for which there seem to be no answers.[19]

Valuing experience

It is common for the dominant group to assume that it understands the experience of an oppressed or non-dominant group. Thus white people are surprised when they realise they do not understand the lives of black people; if they are humbly open and graced with trusted black friends who will speak the truth with them, they may be able to approach understanding by way of their imagination. Similarly there is the assumption that male clergy, preachers, spiritual directors and confessors understand women's experience because – after all – it isn't really so different. By their unwillingness to value their own experience and their silence concerning it, women have contributed to this fallacy.

Considering how inseparable woman's physical being is from her spirituality, it is striking how much of her bodily experience is tabu for open discussion. Menstruation remains relatively

[19] The authors of *Women's Ways of Knowing* note a similar phenomenon in secular higher education: 'The courses are about the culture's questions, questions fished out of the "mainstream" of the disciplines. If the student is female, her questions may differ from the culture's questions, since women, paddling in the bywaters of the culture, have had little to do with positing the questions or designing the agendas of the disciplines' (p. 198).

secret or is mentioned in negative terms such as: does woman's cyclical nature make her unstable and unreliable? Menopause is seen as comic or pathetic, an exception being Margaret Meade's joyous prayer of thanksgiving for the energy and zest of post-menopausal women. Pregnancy and birth are relegated to women's magazines, despite Luke's exemplary theological treatment of the subject. And rarely addressed, in spiritual terms, is women's own deep dislike of their bodies, their dissatifaction with certain features, and their pervasive sense that they need to lose weight, that is, literally diminish themselves. Carried to its extreme, this last-named obsession can lead to death from anorexia. Finally, for too many women, their initial sexual experience is of violation and abuse.

Women's most powerful and formative experiences are often the hidden, secret ones. To the directee they may seem insignificant in the grand scheme of things, hence too homely and earthed for theological reflection with a director. Discussing the relevance of traditional curricula, the authors of *Women's Ways of Knowing* observe: 'The women we interviewed nearly always named out-of-school experiences as their most powerful learning experiences. The mothers usually named childbearing or child rearing.'[20] I would like to rewrite their sentence: the women I interview nearly always name out-of-church experiences as their most powerful theological experiences. Not only do they name childbearing and child rearing; they also name violation and abuse.

In broader terms than the purely physical, women use their own experience to understand the world. Again, their way of cognitive learning in an academic provides a model:

> Most of these women were not opposed to abstraction as such. They found concepts useful in making sense of their experiences, but they balked when the abstractions preceded the experiences or pushed them out entirely. Even the women who were extraordinarily adept at abstract reasoning preferred to start from personal experience.[21]

If women feel safe enough to be themselves, they will approach spiritual direction as an exploration of their experience of God (or their disappointing lack of this experience) rather than an

[20] Belenky *et al.* p. 200.
[21] Ibid. pp. 201–2.

exploration of theological abstractions. Further, the starting point will be the raw material supplied by their own daily life.

There are times when a woman will work more fruitfully with another woman, possibly a lay woman. After all, women talk differently among themselves, as do men. There is, moreover, a special shared understanding between women of common experience: those who have borne children, or widows, or lesbians, for example. While this does not mean that the directee must be matched with her mirror image, she needs as a director someone to whom all aspects of her experience will be acceptable and understandable. But it is equally important to stress that there are many sensitive, imaginative men who meet this requirement. Their very otherness makes them valuable for the woman who is trying to gain a clear perspective. Mindless segregation has no place in spiritual direction, indeed would be a step backward. Men **can** serve as directors for women.

In her fear of seeming trivial and in her undervaluing of her own experience, the directee may avoid topics and areas of deep concern. The spiritual implications of a long and 'uneventful' marriage are often unexplored and underrated. The costs and fruits of faithfulness are not always evident but have a profound effect on the woman's spiritual identity. The spirituality of housework is another neglected area. Most of my male friends and colleagues are unaware of the burden of repetitive menial work that is never done, work that is noticed only when it is neglected. Further, time spent with very young children can simultaneously enrich the spirit, deaden the mind, and tax patience beyond belief. All of this is the raw material of spiritual direction; all of this has a God-component, even though the directee does not see in the minutiae of her life an experience of God.

The director's task is to help the woman find and trust her voice so that her story can be told. To do this is to give her permission to be, discover and reveal her true self. Here, as always, spiritual direction is a ministry of compassionate presence. The directee must be taken seriously, even when she **seems** not to take herself seriously. If the director is to listen critically without pre-judging, it is vital that the director knows his own biases. For example some men should not try to work with well-groomed, well-dressed, middle-class and middle-aged women; unable to see beyond the externals, they are too quick to typecast these women as superficial and materialistic. Similarly an extreme feminist might have little understanding of a dedicated stay-at-home mother, just as the recently divorced woman might see her directee's commitment to a difficult marriage as pathological.

Taking everything seriously, the director never condescends even when the story is told haltingly and without theological sophistication. It is important for director (and directee) to understand that one can talk about 'spiritual' matters without a theological vocabulary. The raw material is there: all that is needed is for the directee to trust her own voice.

The director helps by asking encouraging, 'heart-giving' questions. The right questions can clarify and dispel tentativeness. They can help the woman move away from undue dependence on the authority of others to claim her own innate authority. They can help her uncover and set free her submerged self.

Parzival released the king from his suffering and brought the entire Grail community into harmony and wholeness when he finally asked the simple question: 'Uncle, where do you hurt?' It is such a simple question that the director might forget to ask it, particularly when the woman (or man) sitting opposite seems strong and positive. As traditional care-givers, most women are not prepared for this question although they would expect it from a physician. Socialised to put their own wishes aside (or at least to disguise them), they see the question as an invitation to selfishness or self-indulgence. Instead it is an invitation to **self**: merely naming the source of hurt can expose it to light and air and thereby bring about healing.

Important as this is in all aspects of a woman's life, it is especially critical in the area of spirituality. As she begins to answer the question candidly, she may reveal – to her own surprise – years of denial and years of suppressed pain. The cost of faithfulness has been high, as the woman finds herself able to articulate her grief at her exclusion in religious language and imagery.

A supportive director can help the woman find her place in the communal Christian story. The writings of Elisabeth Moltmann-Wendel, Phyllis Trible and Elisabeth Schuessler-Fiorenza are a valuable resource for the director and in some cases for the directee. Most effective, however, is 'simply' reading the gospels with a woman's eye – men can do this too – attentive to what is not said and, more strikingly, to what is rarely addressed in sermons and teaching. One example must suffice, but there are many, once the reader has become attentive. (This way of reading scripture is not unlike the children's puzzles, where squirrels or rabbits are hidden in a picture. Once you get the hang of it, you find them in the treetops, upside down in the river, disguised among the flowers, everywhere.)

I have conducted a number of retreats on 'The Women around Jesus'.[22] In one of the first gatherings I ask the retreatants (usually women) to retell from memory the story of the woman who anointed Jesus. Unfailingly the group effort reproduces Luke's version: 'a woman of the city, who was a sinner . . . standing behind him at his feet, weeping . . . began to wet his feet with her tears, and wiped them with the hair of her head, and kissed his feet, and anointed them with the ointment'.[23] Then I remind them of Mark's telling of the story: 'a woman came with an alabaster flask of ointment of pure nard, very costly, and she broke the flask and poured it over his head'.[24] We sit for a moment with the picture of these two women, our sisters: the (presumably sexual) sinner crouched weeping on the floor and the unnamed woman standing tall, a prophet anointing a king. Then we smile and weep simultaneously at the irony of Jesus' words about the latter: 'Wherever the gospel is preached in the whole world, what she has done will be told in memory of her.'

Further the director can encourage women (and men) to be comfortable with feminine imagery for God in prayer. This may simply be a matter of 'giving permission' or possibly a brief recounting of the director's own experience. To reassure the anxious or uncertain, he can point out often-overlooked feminine imagery in scripture. (The hidden midwife in Psalm 22:9 was a joyful discovery for me: 'yet you [God] are he who took me out of the womb, and kept me safe upon my mother's breast'.) I like to encourage experimentation and freedom in solitary prayer time, which can often be combined comfortably with traditional corporate worship.

A woman must be willing to embrace risk if she is to push out the boundaries, find her true self and voice, and thereby grow into her own mature spirituality. It is easier not to face the realisation that one's icons have become idols and must be put away, not to accept that one's vision of God has been

---

[22] Elisabeth Moltmann-Wendel's gifted book obviously provided the stimulus: *Women Around Jesus: Reflections on Authentic Personhood*, tr. J. Bowden (SCM Press, 1982).

[23] Luke 7:36–50.

[24] Mark 14:3–9.

constricted and distorted. Madonna Kolbenschlag speaks of
the 'moment of atheism', when the woman lets go of her outgrown faith, ceasing to rely on 'authorities' and trusting herself.[25] In my own more homely idiom, she takes off the training
wheels and discovers to her amazement that the spiritual
bicycle remains upright.

'What do you want?' is another growth-promoting, albeit difficult question since women are acculturated not to want anything. Of course, they **do** 'want' something, unless they have
become emotionally and spiritually numb, but they must be
persuaded that it is permissible to express those wants directly.
The director needs to be gently tenacious in the face of great
resistance: 'I want only God's will' or 'I want only what is best
for my husband, parents, or children' or baldly 'I have no right
to want anything; that would be selfish.' It may help for the
director to point out the pitfalls of manipulative behaviour that
can result from such strenuous selflessness. Scripture is also
helpful: the neglected stories of the importunate widow's harassment of the unjust judge (Luke 18:1–8) and the friend who
keeps knocking on the door at midnight (Luke 11:5–13) give
permission to those who feel they have no right to ask for anything.

The eighth deadly sin

We 'know' from struggling through *Paradise Lost* that THE sin
is overweening pride. (I would vote for idolatry or greed in our
gluttonous society, but Milton speaks for tradition.) The time
I have spent listening to women's stories has convinced me that
there are distinctly feminine patterns of sinfulness, and that
pride is not women's besetting sin, even though many think so
and readily accuse themselves. Not untypically, they are con-
fessing the 'wrong thing'; and even as they talk of pride they are
feeling worthless and powerless.

Women's patterns of sinning are different from men's, but
this does not mean that women are somehow purer or more
holy. However, the model of the woman too good to live, the
doomed heroine of the nineteenth-century novel, has been
internalised with tragic consequences. Embracing the role of
victim is a way of remaining 'sinless', yet this very willingness

[25] Madonna Kolbenschlag, *Kiss Sleeping Beauty Good-Bye*, pp. 185–7.

to let oneself be hurt or even destroyed is a striking example of an essentially sinful way of being.

Far from pride, women's distinctive sin is self-contempt. This self-hatred is symbolised by and centred on the body. I have already noted women's dissatisfaction with their physical selves; studies have shown this to be a peculiarly feminine pre-occupation. Cultural messages are not helpful; for example, to hear repeatedly that 'That ugly flab is you' can only reinforce the idea that one needs to disappear or at least diminish. The potentially fatal disorders of anorexia and bulimia represent the logical consequences of this self-hatred carried to the extreme.

Perhaps most often women's self-contempt manifests itself in an unwillingness to grow, to take the risks that growth demands. It is often difficult for women to see that their reluc-tance to accept maturity is a tacit refusal of their adult responsibility. 'How can this be?' they ask, as they feel them-selves burdened, indeed overwhelmed by their responsibilities as wives, mothers, employees and professionals. Yet by over-responsibility in their obligations to others (especially husbands and children) and by concomitant neglect of themselves, they have managed to avoid inner growth. There is no quality of careless abandon in this spiritual irresponsi-bility; on the contrary it is grim and confining.

Women's tentativeness, already noted, is another mainfest-ation of self-contempt, as is an apparent absorption in triviality. Both are a noisy kind of silence, a screen thrown up – perhaps unconsciously – against clarity. By hesitating to take a firm stand or even expressing herself in decisive language, she is sending a strong message that she does not deserve to be heard. By letting herself become immersed in trivialities she sends a message that she does not deserve to be seen, at least not as a conscious adult. Further, absorption in trivialities deadens pain; for the woman is too fully occupied to face herself, her human relationships, and – of course – God.

Tentativeness may also be a result of a mistaken understand-ing of anger; a kind of clenched-teeth sweet rage is another. Women especially are socialised to believe that anger *per se* is avoidable and wrong and that its expression is sinful. (The word 'sin' is rare in our secular vocabulary; but the phenom-enon is known, dreaded and punishable.) As a result a great deal of spiritual energy goes into combating the 'wrong' sin, and the potentially constructive use of anger is neglected. The result is hurtful and destructive to the woman and to those around her. A woman from my nursing home chaplaincy is etched in my mind: Emma spent her last months filled equally with rage and cancer. Her rigid piety made it impossible for her to question God's purpose, let alone express anger at him. Outwardly sweet and always courteous to her visitors, she made life hell for the uneducated and poorly-paid women who were her caretakers. She died without being able to face the deep wells of anger within herself.[26]

The denial and relinquishing of a woman's own authority inevitably manifests itself as passivity, not the passivity of a healthy self open and empty to receive the Holy Spirit, but rather a leaden inertia. Without discounting the biochemical, genetic, and neurological causes, it seems clear that at least **some** depression is of spiritual origin. Similarly the passivity of self-contempt can reveal itself in addictions, the obvious ones of food, pills and alcohol as well as the less obvious ones of sleep, hyperactivity and consumerism. The last-named is especially insidious since it is culturally reinforced and stimulated.

It is important not to minimise the sin of self-hatred and self-contempt. It **is** a sin, for at its heart is a denial of God's love and the goodness of God's Creation. Pride plays a part after all, for the woman discounts herself as part of Creation and assumes that the rules of divine love do not apply to her. Love is there for everyone else, but not for her.

Like all sin, this cannot be private, hurting the sinner alone. The ramifications touch others, in the woman's immediate circle and beyond. There is the waste of gifts that have not been used, frequently not even acknowledged, coupled with the inability to receive the gifts of others. Self-contempt is a loveless field that offers prime growing conditions to other sins, among them false humility, envy, manipulativeness and sloth. Sloth is an especially sneaky sin, since it can disguise itself in busyness. Here again absorption in trivialities is a symptom.

The director's task is to listen and to detect patterns of self-deception, for women's ways of sinning depend on obfuscation. My two favourite questions – 'What do you want?' and 'Where do you hurt?' – are excellent diagnostic tools for getting at sinful ways and at the same time for revealing the innate beauty and goodness which the woman is denying.

---

[26] Less poignant but equally memorable is the character Ferovius from Shaw's *Androcles and the Lion.* As he bashes everyone who crosses his path, he observes, 'I used to get angry before I became a Christian.'

The director should guard against joining her in trivialis-
ation of herself. A sense of sin is to be taken seriously, for it is a
heavy burden on the directee. It is no comfort to be told 'Oh,
that's not really very important' or, worse still, to be dismissed
with a patronising smile. Even when a sense of sin is misplaced
or misguided, it is a sign that something is wrong and a possible
mask for sinful ways of being. Many women come to spiritual
direction prepared, even eager to believe the worst about themselves. Shame caused by hurt inflicted upon them is easily confused with guilt for which they are responsible.

Some women suffer from a pervasive sense of guilt and sin
simply because they ARE. This is rarely conscious or articulated, but it is crippling. The most striking example in my
experience came in a conversation with Grace, an intelligent
woman of great probity, whose jealous supervisor had accused
her of financial wrongdoing in management of her department.
Almost in despair she protested, 'I didn't do it. I never even
thought about the possibilities for corruption. I know she's [the
supervisor] crazy. So why do I feel so guilty?' Similarly, Allie
found herself singled out for small, cruel practical jokes by a
member of staff of her school. Instead of openly expressed
anger, her response was acceptance of her own guilt: 'I must
have done something; I must have hurt him somehow.' Even
more tragically, the phenomenon of the victims of rape and
sexual abuse blaming themselves is well documented.

Avoiding judgmentalism and condescension, the director
can help the woman separate the strands of her sin/illness. The
author of *The Cloud of Unknowing* aptly observes that sin is a
lump.[27] We need to differentiate the lump and understand its
chemical composition. It very likely contains a lot of inert
matter and perhaps even something of value. The director
assists in separating the good from the bad, the significant from
the insignificant. It is delicate and gentle work, for sin always
involves hurt: hurt of others, hurt of God, hurt of ourselves. The
director helps to pick all this apart and to find the REAL sin.

A special population: survivors of abuse

The whole area of sexuality and sexual experience is a delicate
one. The directee often tends to compartmentalise her life,
assuming that deep concerns in this area are not suitable

[27] *The Cloud*, p. 99.

material for discussion in this context. Regardless of the particular issue – sexual orientation, rape, incest, illegitimate births and abortions – it may take a long time for the real issues to surface. For both director and directee, this is a time of testing and reaching out. When I sense that much is being left unsaid and a great piece of the picture is missing, I probe a little: 'Tell me about your family.' or 'Do you live alone?' I must be prepared for disappointment; such enquiries may not lead anywhere, initially. The directee may not exhibit the discomfort that often accompanies denial or evasion: there is simply no information forthcoming.

The directee naturally feels concern: will I be accepted? Or shamed? Sometimes she asks this question directly, as Beth did at our first meeting: 'I'm a lesbian. Is that going to bother you?' I assured her that it wouldn't, but invited her to let me know if, at any point, I bothered **her**. Of course the deeper and not yet articulated question is, 'Does God accept me?' This is no occasion for polite hypocrisy. It is a good rule not to accept a directee if you cannot be compassionate and hence are in danger of judgmentalism or contempt.

Over the past years I have found myself doing spiritual direction with increasing numbers of women who have survived incest. They are a special group among my directees, with a distinctive spirituality. Those with whom I have worked most closely have given me permission and encouragment to write about our relationship. Because there is so much shame connected with abuse and because the material is so laden, I have changed or omitted non-relevant details. 'Linda' is a composite. Everything I say about her is true, but she cannot be linked to one individual.

In the past ten years scientific studies and first-hand accounts of sexual abuse have proliferated. It is now commonly accepted in the USA that one woman in four has been violated: this can range from rape to isolated instances of improper touch or fondling. (Verbal violation, still mistakenly believed by some men to be flattering to a woman, is not included.) One in ten is or has been the victim of ongoing sexual abuse. These are conservative figures.

While there are male victims of sexual abuse, this is typically a crime and sin against girl-children. The myth of the dangerous stranger is just that: the woman who has been sexually abused is usually the victim of a known and trusted person – her father (most often), uncle, grandfather, mother's boyfriend, or brother. In sibling incest, unless there is great discrepancy in size, there is a **slight possibility** that the relationship is consensual (I do not here minimise the seriousness of sibling incest and its potential, painful consequences for the adult woman). In all other cases there is coercion. Even though the coercion is not always physical, it is an act of spiritual and emotional violence.

There are no statistics available, but these survivors seem drawn to the Church. Sometimes, they tell me, it was the only safe place in a nightmarish childhood. Sometimes they experience real grace in a sense of God's love – in spite of everything. I would be reluctant ever to dismiss their devotion as denial or compensation although it is undeniable that religion can be used to escape reality.

When some incest survivors come to spiritual direction they are genuinely unaware of their own painful history. Because their memories are too overwhelming, amnesia is a means of survival. Years of incest and rape are not a part of their consciousness until, in middle age, they begin to recall. Memory may return gradually or suddenly. At this point spiritual direction is not enough; it is only one component in the woman's work towards wholeness. She urgently needs psychotherapeutic help from a specially trained person or one who is, at least, highly sensitive to issues of sexual abuse. In most cases she should work with a woman, at least initially. There are also support groups and twelve-step programmes; these can be helpful after a period of intensive individual psychotherapy and in conjunction with it. I am most comfortable working in cooperation with the psychotherapist, with the directee acting as go-between. Unless the directee initiates it, I have no actual contact with the psychotherapist. (I have never met Linda's therapist, but I feel great affection and respect for her. Linda regularly conveys our greetings to one another.)

Before recall, the abuse survivor may seem to be functioning adequately. But she may also seem talkative, even shallow; her preoccupation with triviality is like a bandage covering her painful wound.[28] A number of my directees have been drawn

---

[28] Otherwise sympathetic writers judge women are judged severely if not harshly for their 'triviality', failing to see that it can be a means of coping, even survival. For examples, see J. Neville Ward, *The Following Plough*, p. 100; Martin Smith, *Reconciliation*, p. 78; and Wendy M. Wright, *The Feminist Mystic*, p. 111.

instinctively to the pain of others, hence they are much concerned with 'good works' and 'helping others'.

The director needs to be patient, allowing time for trust to
build up. Even as they reach out for support and understanding, there is no reason for these women to trust **anyone**. For the
most part, they are skilled at coping (that is, the survivors are
skilled at coping; the less able may be dead, chemically
addicted, or institutionalised). But this is often on a superficial
level, and a long time is required to get past courteous
banalities.

Unless the director knows where to look, there is often no
obvious clue to the pain and inner turmoil. I am developing
a sixth – and at this point indefinable – sense of the special
woundedness of the abused. However it is especially important
to tread softly if the person is in a state of amnesia; and I may
know intuitively more than I need or should articulate to the
directee. At most I permit myself a gentle invitation to go
deeper: 'I sense that you have been hurt a lot.'

When the directee has begun to recall her earlier experience,
there is a continued need for patience. As more material sur-
faces, the direction relationship grows in trust, and the directee
moves towards some kind of healing. Sometimes it feels as if we
are gradually peeling off layers of concealment; at others, it is
like going ever deeper down a spiral staircase. As in all direction
relationships, but here especially, confidentiality must be
impeccable.

The victim is filled with shame; and almost always there is
the typical confusion of guilt and shame: she feels somehow to
blame for what was done to her. Also, as she moves towards
greater healing and its concomitant awareness, she is frightened by glimpses of her own deep rage and her fear of what
might happen if that rage were expressed.

In working with survivors of sexual abuse there are no short
cuts. The spiritual director must scrupulously avoid 'shoulds'
and 'oughts', with one exception. I remember saying to Linda,
'Most of the time I will be careful not to tell you what you
should do. But there is one thing you **must** do, and I will keep
at you about it: value yourself!' The survivor feels devalued and
sullied; she cannot be told too often that she is worthy of love
and respect. (At my suggestion, Linda took as her mantra 'I
am clean!' She wove the words into her prayers, taped them on
her mirror, and clung to them when shame threatened to flood
over her.)

Occasionally I receive referrals from psychotherapists. An abuse survivor is crushed by her shame and feeling of uncleanness. If it is in accordance with her religious tradition, the therapist feels that she might be helped by the sacrament of reconciliation. These are poignant confessions, not to be hurried. Even though she knows intellectually that she was betrayed and violated, the woman feels compelled to blame herself. Moreover, she is sure that the rage welling up in her is a confirmation of her sinfulness. We talk about her anger and how it can be a source of sin or great constructive energy. The woman has undoubtedly already heard this from her psychotherapist, but it is good news when told afresh in a religious setting. Technically, I should withhold absolution because I have heard the story of the victim, not the perpetrator; but this is not the time for a legalistic approach to the sacraments. The woman's relief is almost palpable when I place my hands on her head and say, 'The Lord has put away all your sins. Go in peace.' I will probably never see her again.

The greatest gift the director can bring is a loving presence. While it is important to maintain detachment, a deep emotionl involvement is also inevitable and desirable. I have already told of Linda's response to my tears, which I had hoped to whisk away before she could see them. As memories come flooding back, the director may hear of horror and degradation beyond belief. As one survivor told me, 'I have been in Auschwitz.' And she had. In critical times I break my rule about limiting conversations between regular meetings. I invited this woman to call me at any time, day or night, until this particularly painful period had been lived through. She accepted the invitation but never abused my hospitality.

The director needs to find some way of dealing with her own reactions to the painful material. If she herself has been abused, she may be tempted to identify too closely with the directee, even to the point of appropriating the other woman's pain. On the other hand, if she has had a warm, healthy relationship with her father and the other significant men in her life, it may be difficult to believe that families are capable of intentional cruelty to their most helpless members. In any event, dealing with her own emotions is a delicate process because the directee's confidences must be protected. Conversation with her own director can help restore perspective, as long as she is careful to concentrate on her own reactions and not on the raw material of the survivor's story. Keeping the journal is invaluable. And of course the director prays, as always, for those who trust her, and for herself. I realise that when I pray for Linda she has become for me a symbol or representative of all women and children suffering abuse.

Here again there are no short cuts. This can be heavy, lonely work. After doing spiritual direction with a number of abuse survivors, I know things that I would rather not know, and I have glimpsed depths whose existence I would prefer to deny.

At all times the director needs to be credulous. The abuse did happen! We are still suffering from Freud's inability to deal with the real experience of upper-middle-class little girls in turn-of-the-century Vienna and hence to believe their stories. If the directee said it happened, IT HAPPENED. And it is still happening: even after decades of amnesia, flashes of recollection have an almost unbearable immediacy.

It may be impossible for a man to work with an abused woman, at least in the early stages of her growing consciousness. One directee, whose appearance and manner give no clue to her painful history, has told me of her difficulty at the Exchange of the Peace during the Eucharist; for a long time, she tried to position herself so that she would not have to touch and be touched by a man. It is not surprising that she and other survivors would be ill at ease with a male director. (I have noted one exception: gay men, who themselves have received societal abuse, often have surprising rapport with survivors of incest and other sexual abuse.) It must be difficult for compassionate men not to take this rejection personally. At later stages, their supportive male presence can greatly advance healing; but until then they must be content to wait. (Male directors are, of course, needed to work with male survivors of sexual abuse and with the abusers themselves. I have done direction with male survivors, but thus far no abuser has identified himself.)

The survivors of sexual abuse have the difficult task of getting it all together. Understandably they are even more likely than others to fall prey to the common tendency to separate the 'spiritual' from what has really happened in their lives. God-talk may be infrequent or voluble but unconnected with reality. In either case, I ask from time to time: 'Where was God when this was happening to you? Where is God now? Do you feel angry with God?' They are often afraid to express the possibility of anger with God, having a tendency to excuse him as if his attention had merely wandered during their ordeal. (Some Germans in the Third Reich behaved similarly when they learned of atrocities. Surely their leader had not known that such things were going on, otherwise they would have been stopped. The expression, '*Wenn das der Fuehrer wuesste!*' 'If our leader only knew!' became a cliché and eventually a grim joke.) Along with this unwillingness to face squarely the presence or absence of God, most abuse survivors are equally unable to confront the probable complicity of their mothers. At least in early stages, it is more bearable to see the father (or brother, uncle or grand-father) as acting in isolation. Eventually they come to share the insight of Elie Wiesel and other Holocaust survivors whose faith was forged in suffering: God was there, in the suffering.

These are courageous women. I have learned a great deal about praying with and from them. The Psalms are a source of strength for them, especially Psalm 22 (My God, my God, why have you forsaken me? And are so far from my cry and from the words of my distress); and Psalm 88 (O Lord, my God, my Saviour, by day and night I cry to you). The imprecatory psalms are often a surprise to women schooled in niceness; I encourage them to read and savour the angry parts our lection-ary has excluded. For example, verses 22–28 of Psalm 69 are a fine example of unbridled rage:

> Let the table before them be a trap
>   and their sacred feasts a snare.
> Let their eyes be darkened, that they may not see,
>   and give them continual trembling in their loins.
> Pour out your indignation upon them,
>   and let the fierceness of your anger overtake them.
> Let their camp be desolate,
>   and let there be none to dwell in their tents. . .
> Lay to their charge guilt upon guilt,
>   and let them not receive your vindication.
> Let them be wiped out of the book of the living
>   and not be written among the righteous.

If the Psalmist could urge God to wreak terrible vengeance on his adversaries, the survivor of abuse can permit herself a little anger. She can write it, speak it or shout it.

I encourage prayers of petition for understanding, strength and restored health. But I am cautious about the danger of prematurity in prayers of forgiveness. Again and again the sur-vivor says, 'I know I should forgive my father, but . . .' Or even more painfully, 'My mother and the whole family tell me that

I should be willing to forgive and forget.' The wound of abuse is like any other deep and infected wound. If the surface is allowed to heal over too quickly, poison remains to spread sickness deep within. So I counsel the directee to pray to want to be able to forgive – some day.

I have already touched upon the healing power of sacramental confession, even when the penitent is more burdened by shame than by guilt. It is helpful for the director to point out the difference, in no way minimising the tremendous burden of shame. The privacy of the confessional might be the only place where the directee feels safe to articulate it and to dispel its power by naming it directly. It helps restore perspective when I ask, 'Where is your sin in this?' or 'Where is the potential for sin?' Both are there, but rarely in the ways assumed by the abuse survivor.

It goes without saying that I am cautious about paternal imagery in prayer, for example in the use of the Our Father. To avoid the possibility of unwittingly inflicting more pain upon her, I am willing to be led by the directee, who may find in God the loving father she has not known on earth, or may prefer to separate herself as far as possible from all parental imagery.

Finally the woman who has survived sexual abuse often develops into a powerful intercessor. It does not happen easily or quickly: at first she must deal intensively with her own experiences, then with those of women and children whose suffering has been similar. As she perseveres she often finds in herself wells of compassion for **all** victims.

EPILOGUE

And he came to her and said, 'Hail, O favoured one, the Lord is with you!' But she was greatly troubled at the saying, and considered in her mind what sort of greeting this might be. (Luke 1:28–29)

Listen, my son [daughter] to your master's precepts, and incline the ear of your heart. (Prologue to the Rule of St Benedict)

For God alone my soul waits in silence; from him comes my salvation. (Psalm 62:1)

And the Lord called Samuel again the third time. And he arose and went to Eli, and said, 'Here am I, for you called me.' Then Eli perceived that the Lord was calling the boy. Therefore Eli said to Samuel, 'Go, lie down; and if he calls you, you shall say, "Speak, Lord, for thy servant hears." ' (1 Samuel 3:8–9)

. . . a cloud came and overshadowed them; and they were afraid as they entered the cloud. And a voice came out of the cloud, saying, 'This is my Son, my Chosen; listen to him!' (Luke 9:34–35)

WRITING A BOOK about spiritual direction is a presumptuous act: one sets oneself up as an authority. Perhaps one is even taken seriously and becomes raw material for footnotes! Yet I am still working on my definition of spiritual direction, playing with images and models, and ever more aware that whatever a spiritual director is – I am not there yet. Increasingly I rejoice in my amateur status and pray God I never lose it.

The amateur is a lover. Love impels her work and lies at its heart. Spiritual direction, as a work of love, is also a work of freedom. The director is willing to let be, to love with an open hand. Hers is a contemplative love, immune from temptation to devour, possess or manipulate. Always seeing the other as a child of God, she is filled with respect, even awe, in the presence of the person sitting across the sacred space – be it my holy patch of worn carpet or at the other end of a park bench.

Willing to let go and let be, the director is unwilling to despair. He has faith in the process of growth and change – and even more faith in the power of God's grace. This is a ministry of hope and newness, a never-ending newness which enlivens and even helps define the status of the amateur. The professional works according to standard procedures – when I visit my ophthalmologist or my dentist for a regular examination, I have come to know the routine. When I spend an hour in spiritual direction – sitting on either side of the sacred space – I am much less certain what will happen. Even in the security and comfort of a long-standing relationship when rhythms and rituals are well established, each meeting is new. The amateur-director must be ready for the unexpected; for despite all our attempts to domesticate him God deals in surprises. Yet, as I noted in the beginning, most of us don't really like surprises; there is great comfort in predictable blandness.

But from the days of Abraham, God's messengers have a way of turning up in unlikely places and at unlikely times. When I read Luke's account of the Annunciation and manage to put aside the pretty pictures that clutter my imagination, I am astonished by the overwhelming terror of this story of the inbreaking of the unexpected. Luke tells us that Mary was 'greatly troubled' at the angel's greeting – and well she might be! What a masterpiece of understatement! Mary might well have preferred an ordinary day, to have passed the betrothal period placidly and then to have married Joseph and had a nice ordinary family.

But instead she received a momentous greeting.

Along with the empty tomb, the Annunciation is the story of ultimate surprise: God's messenger – often well disguised and quite unlikely – breaks into the routine of the ordinary and the predictable, and announces the divine presence among and within us. Sometimes I ask myself and my directees: what would you do if an angel were waiting in the back seat of your car or in your office or maybe at home in your kitchen? You, with a deadline to meet; or a spouse who is demanding not equal time but a little space in your life; or maybe a sick child; or perhaps a critical encounter with your boss looming up in the very near future. Or maybe you're tired, at the edge of burnout, and plan to spend two or three glorious hours letting your mind go pleasantly numb before the TV. And you hear: 'Hail, O favoured one, the Lord is with you. Have I got a deal for YOU!'

Spiritual direction is about entertaining angels, troublesome and unpredictable angels who turn up at surprising and rarely convenient times and places. Spiritual direction is about recognising those angels and helping our sisters and brothers who entrust themselves to us to be joyously attentive at those small annunciations, those times when God's messenger breaks into their lives and says: Hail, O favoured one, get ready to be shaken up. Get ready to make a place for him in your soul and in your life.

The annunciations that come to us don't always look or feel like good news. Indeed they may feel like blows or set-backs, interruptions and intrusions into our tidy, well-planned lives. Occasionally the news is joyous and clear, but the annunciation can take the form of downright bad news: illness, rejection, bereavement, seeming loss and waste.

The God who surprises uses strange, unlikely, even dubious material – including those of us who practise the ministry of spiritual direction. The God who surprises wastes nothing, including our 'mistakes'. I look back on incidents of my own ineptness being graciously rescued and transformed, with the gratitude and amazement felt by one who has unconsciously danced on the edge of an abyss. Again and again I am struck by the power of this ministry, made fruitful by our mutual faithfulness and by God's economy: words which seemed to me banal and inadequate have had meaning for the directee, and silence born of my incompetence has become rich and deep.

Then I remember the fearsome Mrs G of my hospital ministry, her dismissal of me as an agent of change, my summary relegation to amateur status: 'You mean you just walk around and listen to people?' And I realise, 'That's what I do.' More than host, teacher or midwife, as a spiritual director I am a holy listener.

Listen is such a little, ordinary word. Like many little, ordinary words, it is easily passed over. Yet we all know the pain of not being listened to, of not being heard. I feel a clutch at my heart whenever I see a child desperate, inarticulate with grief, crying for his preoccupied parent to listen to him. My vicarious anguish seemed excessive, until I realised that I am that child and that I fear the awful emptiness when a voice goes unheard. Munch and Siquieros have captured this terrible isolation in their paintings. And all of us, if we delve into memory, have experienced it.

In a way, not to be heard is not to be. This can be the plight of the very young and the very old, the very sick, the 'confused', and all too frequently the dying – literally no one in their lives has time or patience to listen. Or perhaps we lack courage to hear them. As time-obsessed people, we dismiss those not 'worth' listening to.

By contrast the holy listener is reluctant to classify and then to dismiss another person. As an amateur and open to surprises, he makes a willing gift of his attentiveness. At present this gift is all too rare, as spiritual directors remain in short supply. Many people have found a substitute in psychotherapy: ironically, ours is the first culture that pays others to listen to us. Perhaps it is time for amateurs to reclaim their calling. Since even the most limited among us can be a spiritual friend, I find myself wondering what would happen if we all cultivated holy listening. The world might well be transformed!

We forget how intimate listening is. It is alive and fluid in its mutuality. There is interaction, even if no one moves a muscle and even if the listener says nothing. Vulnerability is shared when silence is shared.

Holy listening is a work of mutual obedience. It is important to remember the link between the root word, *audire*, and the much maligned and misunderstood virtue of obedience: to be obedient is to listen, to hear. It bears no relation to Pavlovian reflexes or to cringing servility. Both the director and the directee are listening and hearing, attentive and respectful. Spiritual directors can find a model in the story of the child Samuel and the priest Eli.[1] It is comforting to remember that Eli – who is wise, experienced and attentive – nevertheless misses the point twice. And even more comforting to remember that the Lord keeps calling until his voice is both heard and recognised. Both Eli and Samuel, director and directee, are enmeshed in listening; each to his truest self, avoiding the snares of self-deception; to the other, in mutually covenanted obedience; and ultimately to God. Here the director/Eli brings the gift of discernment that comes with detachment.

We can be Elis for our directees. We can listen and help them to listen for the voice of God in scripture, dreams, the words

[1] 1 Samuel 3:1–18.

of friends – and enemies, 'what they knew all along'. We can encourage them to go trustfully into a dark place and wait: Go, lie down, and if he calls you, you shall say, 'Speak, Lord, for thy servant hears.' We can listen with them in darkness, suffering and solitude and then help them understand what they have heard. Eli guided Samuel at great cost to himself. It is unlikely that the ministry of spiritual direction will make such drastic demands on its practitioners, but we would do well to emulate Eli in his willingness to put self aside.

When both director and directee are mutually obedient and engaged in holy listening, **the story gets told**. Too often we become isolated both from our own story and the Christian story and consequently are dominated by affliction or relationships or work. Separated from our true context, we can be overcome by our present situation – even when it is basically 'good' and when we feel that God has called us to it. (For example, I have known seminarians become inundated by the tasks and deadlines pressing upon them. Superficially they are performing well, but they have lost touch with themselves and the voice which called them.)

Separated from our stories, we lose our identity. In my initial days working as a chaplain in the nursing home, I despaired of ever distinguishing one patient from another. Old and frail, propped or strapped into wheelchairs, they lined the long corridors of the skilled nursing floors. Like prisoners and refugees, they all looked alike. I was able to see them as persons, children of God, only when I was willing to be a holy listener and to be present at their sometimes halting and incoherent telling of the story. Telling the story restores us to personhood and identity – our true identity in Christ – and thereby restores us to context and context to us.

As a holy listener – the listening is holy, I am still me – I have to put myself out of the way, to become humble in the true sense of knowing my place in the order of God's creation. I must be disinterested, critical without being judgmental. And above all I must be reverent, for I am entrusted with something precious and tender. As the stories are told, the vulnerability of both director and directee is apparent as masks fall off or are put aside. The director is invited to share in pain, hunger, courage, hope, joy and holiness.

The holy listener is subject to a variety of temptations: always to have a (presumably) wise response; to understand, evaluate and interpret **everything**; to keep the conversation lively as if a spiritual direction meeting were a non-alcoholic and holy cocktail party; and – most insidious of all – to be interesting. (I was simultaneously touched and amused by a note from a directee who thanked me for my 'blessed centredness'; filled with ego-laden performance anxiety, I had been almost certain that he found me hopelessly dull!)

Coming without an agenda, the holy listener is open to anything the directee might bring. She is willing to hear about darkness and desolation, the times of God's seeming absence and neglect. She is not frightened by another's anger, doubt or fear; and she is comfortable with tears. At the same time, the holy listener knows the truth of the resurrection.

This ministry of presence is a kind of living out of intercessory prayer, as the holy listener waits and watches – sometimes in the warmth of the stable, sometimes in the pure white light on the high mountain apart, sometimes in desolation at the foot of the cross, and sometimes with fear and great joy in the encounter with the risen Christ.